Standard Grade
English

Frank Fitzsimons ✕ John Mannion

with contributions from Larry Flanagan

Contents

Writing skills

Writing

Reading: Responding To Literature

Reading: Prose

Reading: Drama

Reading: Poetry

Talking

Examinations

Standard Grade

It is important to know what is expected of you. This page shows you how the English course is structured, how to do extra study for folio pieces and how to begin revision for examinations.

English

In English you will be given a grade in **reading**, **writing** and **talking**. These three elements are of equal value, contributing one-third each towards your overall grade.

Coursework accounts for two-thirds of your final grade: half of your **reading** and **writing** grades come from your folio; all of your **talking** grade is assessed in class.

Reading – folio

You are required to submit **three critical evaluations on texts** you have studied during your two-year course. Two must be from **prose**, **drama** and **poetry**, and the third can be from any genre, including **media**, or it could be an **imaginative response** to a text.

Talking

Talk is graded through a series of targeted assessments in which your teacher will focus on your participation in **group discussions** or the delivery of **individual talks**.

Writing – folio

Your writing folio consists of two pieces of writing. One should be broadly **transactional** / **discursive** in nature (giving information or expressing a point of view); the other should be primarily **expressive** / **imaginative** (a reflection on personal experience while conveying your thoughts and feelings or a specific genre, such as a short story).

Exams

Exams account for **one-third of your final grade** – 50% of your exam assessment is reading and 50% is writing.

Reading exam

Your reading exam consists of **two close reading papers** where you read a passage and then answer questions designed to test your understanding of the material.

Everyone sits the General Paper, which covers Grades 3 and 4. Depending on your potential achievement you either sit the Credit Paper, Grades 1 and 2, or the Foundation Paper, Grades 5 and 6. You will be awarded the highest grade achieved from the two papers you sit.

Writing exam

You are required to select a **single task** from a range of options and produce an essay within one hour and fifteen minutes. Your work is graded from 1 to 7.

Top Tip

Try answering questions against the clock – as the time factor often catches pupils out.

How to begin your revision

Know your course requirements

- If you **know the requirements of the course** then you will stand a much better chance of meeting them.
- Make sure that you **understand how your course is set out**.
- Ask your **teacher for advice** on what you can expect to face in your exams.
- **Look at past exam papers** fairly early in your course, since these will help you to understand what you have to aim for to get a good mark.

Complete your coursework

You cannot get a final grade unless all your folio is completed. You can always submit re-drafted assignments, with your teacher's agreement, to get better grades, providing that you are not overdoing it by racing to catch up with your coursework in several subjects. If you fall behind with your assignments, you risk producing poor ones by rushing them.

Produce an exam revision timetable

- **Time management is crucial** at every stage in your revision, not just in the exams.
- **Leave yourself time to relax** and do not overdo it! If you try too hard, you could end up doing your best work outside the exam room because you are too tired in the exam.
- Go to bed in good time and do not stay up late doing last-minute revision.
- Allow a few days in your revision timetable in which you do nothing at all. You will **recharge your batteries** and be the better for it.
- If you do not understand something, have a short break. Your brain unconsciously puzzles things out while you are doing something else. When you start your revision again the problem may seem simple to solve.
- Doing **a little study often** is better for the mind than doing a lot rarely. That is how people learn foreign languages.

Top Tip

Revise all aspects of punctuation early in your course. This will help you to produce better coursework and it will also give you more confidence for your final exams.

Team work

Pair up with a friend if this helps to motivate you. Why not proof-read each other's work? You will get better at spotting your own mistakes.

Catching up on missing assignments or producing better ones

You may have missed an assignment for a variety of reasons. Maybe you are dissatisfied with a folio assignment that you rushed. Perhaps you thought that you could have done a better assignment. Check with your teacher if you can work on a missed assignment at home or continue to re-draft work until you are satisfied with it. However, your teacher will have to be assured that the final piece is your own work because he or she has to sign a form to this effect for the SQA.

Punctuation again!

You cannot get good grades in English unless you can punctuate your writing skilfully and correctly. You may be still surviving on skills learned in Primary!

Why use punctuation?

- When you speak, you punctuate naturally through your pauses and body language.
- However, **when you write you have to help your reader understand what you mean through a variety of punctuation marks**.
- The more you know about punctuation, the better you will be able to express yourself.
- Pupils who use semi-colons and colons stand out from others, especially if they use these punctuation marks effectively.

Markers can miss good points and ideas in your writing when their attention is continually drawn to punctuation errors.

Clarify ideas

Writing is a second-hand way of getting our meaning across to others; we need to punctuate our work to help our audience understand us.

Remember that when we let our writing pass into the hands of others, our punctuation marks and the words we use are all that there is to communicate our message. We are no longer in a position to correct any errors, as we would be if we were speaking directly to our audience.

To sum up: **we use punctuation marks to clarify** the points and ideas that we want to communicate to others.

Internet

Visit www.leckieandleckie.co.uk for links to helpful sites on punctuation. You'll find the links for the Standard Grade English Success Guides in the Learning Lab section of the site.

Begin all sentences and are used at the beginning of lines of verse.

Are used for **initials of people's names and places**. Remember that 'I' needs a capital letter too.

Are used when you begin **direct speech**; for example: Julia asked, 'Have you begun your revision for English yet?'

Have to be used for adjectives from **proper** (specific) **nouns**; for example: English, French, Elizabethan and McDonalds.

Capital letters

Need to be used in the **first and main words of titles** of books, newspapers, films, groups and programmes, etc.

Are used when writing letters with 'Dear' and 'Yours . . .'.

Are used for **days of the week, months, holidays** and **special days**.

Are used as **acronyms** for organisations; for example: BBC, NATO and GMTV. Note that you do not need a dot after each letter if it is a well-known organisation.

Top Tip
Get into the habit of proof-reading your work. Target the errors that you usually make.

Quick Test

1. Why is punctuation necessary?
2. List four occasions when you would use capital letters.
3. Correct the following sentences:
   a) 'what's the capital of portugal, lauren?'
   b) my favourite song at the moment is 'i knew i loved you' by savage garden.
4. Which words need a capital: hamburger restaurant, monday, summer, the atlantic, westlife, rspca, sea, christmas, louise?

Answers 1. So that you can be clearly understood. **2.** You should use them for titles of books, to introduce speech, in acronyms, as initials, in letters, as adjectives from proper nouns, to begin sentences, and in days, month names and holidays. **3. a)** 'What's the capital of Portugal, Lauren?' **b)** My favourite song at the moment is 'I Knew I Loved You' by Savage Garden. **4.** Monday, Atlantic, Westlife, RSPCA, Christmas and Louise.

Punctuating sentences

Full stops

A **full stop** is the main punctuation mark that **signals the end of one idea and the beginning of another**.

Sentences help to complete ideas in your writing. You can use full stops to make strong points in your writing, because they slow readers down.

Change your sentences by making some long and some short; **variety** helps to keep your audience interested in what you have to say. Try to be **expressive** through your choice of punctuation.

Read your work aloud and listen to where one idea ends and another begins. Each idea is a sentence. Trust your ears.

Top Tip

Select the punctuation mark that best fits the meaning and purpose. The more expressive you are, the better your writing will be.

Semi-colons

Semi-colons join two or more closely related ideas:

- Steve worked hard for his results; he stuck to his revision plan.
- Spring has come early; the trees have begun to blossom and the grassy banks are full of daffodils.

Semi-colons separate sets of items in a list when there are commas within the sets or lists:

- When you unpack your new computer you will find everything you need: multi-coloured leads; the plugs for your monitor and base unit; the speakers with their leads; a microphone, if this is included, with a stand; manuals for your computer and, if you are lucky, lots of interesting software.

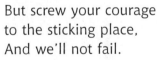

NB: You do not need a capital letter after a semi-colon.

Colons

Colons are two dots, one above the other. They are used to:

- **introduce a list**
  You should bring to your exam: a watch, two pens, a ruler, tissues and hope!

- **introduce quotations**
  Hamlet ponders: 'To be or not to be? That is the question.'
  (It is also acceptable to use a comma here.)

- **expand on the meaning of a previous idea**
  Tracy scored the highest grade in the exam: it was an A*.

A dash can also do the job of a colon by emphasising the sentence that follows:

- Tom had achieved fantastic results in his exams – he got As in five of them.

- **punctuate dialogue in plays**

  Macbeth: If we should fail?
  Lady Macbeth: We fail!
                   But screw your courage
                   to the sticking place,
                   And we'll not fail.

Other punctuation

Exclamation marks

Exclamation marks help to express surprise, anger, fear, joy and most other emotions. For example: Louise! It is good to see you!

Question marks

Look at how professional writers use punctuation as you read their work. Pause over some passages and think about the effectiveness of the punctuation.

Question marks can be used for **rhetorical questions** where no direct reply is expected, only mental agreement; for example: 'Who could defend a statement like that?'

They can also be used for **requests for information**: 'What time is it?'

You do not need a question mark for an indirect question: 'Siobhan asked me for a pen.'

Top Tip

To get high grades in Standard Grade you will need to vary the length of your sentences and the style of your punctuation.

Quick Test

1. Explain one of the things that semi-colons can do.

2. What does a full stop do?

3. Can a colon introduce a list of items?

4. Can colons be used to introduce a quotation?

5. Give one other purpose for a colon.

Answers 1. They link two closely related phrases or separate sets of items in a list where there are commas within the sets. **2.** It marks the end of a sentence. **3.** Yes. **4.** Yes. **5.** It links another phrase which expands upon the meaning of the first, or punctuates dialogue in plays.

Speech marks and commas

The skilful use of punctuation marks can improve your expression

Commas

Commas separate items in lists:

- I would like three hamburgers, a cheeseburger, a large serving of fries and a coffee.

Commas clarify sentences that could be misleading:

- After a period of calm, students returned after the fire alarm.

Commas need to be used in direct speech:

- Elaine was curious about the previous evening and asked, 'Where did you get to?'
  'The shopping centre,' John replied.

Commas can be used to mark off words, phrases, and connectives in sentences:

- Billy, who did not like to be made fun of, was angry.
- On the other hand, there was no harm in what Carly said.

Top Tip

Be careful not to use commas instead of full stops in sentences.

Speech marks

There are four main rules for setting out speech:

1. Use **inverted commas** for the words spoken: Catherine said, 'I haven't seen you in ages!'

2. **Direct speech must be separated from the rest of the writing by a punctuation mark**; see the comma in the example above.

3. Remember to **use a capital letter** when you begin the direct speech: Catherine said, 'It's ages since I last saw you.'

4. Each time you introduce a **new speaker**, begin a new line and indent. That is, begin the speech of your new speaker three letter spaces to the right of the margin.

Quotation marks

- Quotation marks are **inverted commas for words or phrases cited from texts**. Use single inverted commas for speech and double inverted commas for speech within speech. For example: Jane shouted to her husband in the next room, 'Your mother phoned and she said, "When are you going to visit me?" Colin, I thought that you called in on her last week.'

- **Remember to close quotation marks**. It is confusing for readers and markers if you fail to do so! To show that you are ending a quotation, place the final full stop on the outside of the inverted comma; for example: In *My Fair Lady* Eliza Doolittle shows her independence from Professor Higgins when she says, 'I can do without you'.

Eliza Doolittle.

Title marks

- In secondary schools, **inverted commas** are used to signify book titles, stories, newspapers, magazines, television programmes, movies or shows. For example: 'My Fair Lady' is the title of the musical or 1964 film version of the play, 'Pygmalion'.

- In your writing always use title marks to show the difference between **eponymous characters** and the names of the work in which they appear. For example: Macbeth is a character whereas 'Macbeth' is a play. (Eponymous characters share their names with the titles of their texts.)

- The convention (or accepted rule) for titles in universities is to underline them, e.g. <u>Hamlet</u> and <u>Macbeth</u>. The main thing is to **remain consistent** in your method of identifying titles.

- Note that if you use italics for titles then this is acceptable for printed work.

Quick Test

1. Identify three uses for commas.

2. Make up a sentence in which you use all four rules for setting out speech.

3. What do you need to use when you write out the title of a film, book or story?

Answers 1. They can mark off a list and phrases within a sentence; they are used within direct speech. **2.** Phil said, 'Buy the latest team shirt.' / 'It is too expensive,' said Paul. **3.** Title marks, underlining or italics.

Apostrophes

Apostrophes help to show that something belongs to someone (possession) or to shorten words (contraction).

Key Facts

Its and *it's* can be confusing words.
- If you wrote, 'I emptied a box of its contents', you would not need an apostrophe because *its* in this instance is a possessive pronoun.
- If you say, 'It's going to rain all day', you need an apostrophe because you mean *it is*.

Apostrophes of possession

Top Tip

Abbreviated words are only to be used in informal writing. We use them when we speak or write to friends or family. Avoid using shortened words in your assignments and exams unless you are asked to do so.

Possessive pronouns

Pronouns like these do not need apostrophes to show ownership:
- **my**, e.g. The watch is mine.
- **his or hers**, e.g. The computer is hers.
- **yours**, e.g. The bag is yours.
- **its**, e.g. The box was emptied of its contents.
- **ours**, e.g. The car is ours.
- **theirs**, e.g. The house is theirs.

Apostrophes of ownership for one person or thing

If there is a **single owner, place the apostrophe before the 's':**
- Tim's video player
- Christine's house

Apostrophes of ownership for more than one owner

If there is **more than one owner**, you need to **put the apostrophe after the 's'** to show that you mean a plural owner:
- The Jacksons' video
- The Smiths' house

If a person's name already ends in 's', you can do one of two things:
- James's haircut or James' haircut

Whichever style you go for, remain consistent.

If a plural noun does not need an 's' to make it plural, you should place your apostrophe before the 's':
- The men's business venture
- The children's playground
- The women's society
- The people's champion

Expression

You can **vary your expression by using an apostrophe**. For example, 'The claws of the cat' becomes 'The cat's claws' with an apostrophe.

If you are unsure of whether to use a possessive apostrophe then write your sentence the long way round. For example, 'Dan's new house' becomes 'The new house of Dan'.

Always ask yourself why you are inserting an apostrophe. Do not put it in just for good measure.

Apostrophes of contraction

Apostrophes are used to show that one or more letters have been missed out.

Contractions combine two words into one with an apostrophe.

- I'm = I am
- They're = They are
- Won't = Will not
- Doesn't = Does not
- Can't = Cannot
- Would've = Would have

Top Tip
Apostrophes are marks that help readers to understand the intention of the writer. Use them to convey meaning as fully as you can.

Apostrophes when writing the time or dates

- 'I will see Dave at 7 o'clock.' This is the short way of writing 'seven of the clock'.

Missing numbers in dates can be suggested by an apostrophe:

- 21st of September '99
- 3rd of November '01

Apostrophes in plays

Playwrights such as Shakespeare shortened their words to allow their verse to remain in **iambic pentameter**. Shakespeare tried to divide his blank-verse lines into ten syllables, that is, five feet of two syllables each.

Take this example from *Romeo and Juliet*, in which Romeo wants Juliet to exchange vows:

- Romeo: 'Th' exchange of thy love's faithful vow for mine.'

Apostrophes in dialect

Apostrophes are used a great deal by writers when they try to represent local dialect:

- ' 'ow's it goin' me ole mate?'

William Shakespeare

Quick Test

True or false?

1. Possessive pronouns can take apostrophes.
2. Apostrophes lengthen words.
3. Apostrophes can help to show ownership.
4. If a person's name ends with an 's', you can put the apostrophe after it.
5. I ca'nt is correct.
6. Apostrophes of possession can help to vary your sentences and make them shorter.

Sentences

Sentence types

Sentences can be put into four groups according to what they do. They can be **statements** (which give information), **exclamations** (e.g. My Goodness!), **instructions or commands** (e.g. Insert your card this way up.) or **questions**. Sentences are also grouped into structures: simple, compound, complex and minor.

1. **Simple sentences** must contain:
   - **a subject** (what / who does the action)
   - **a verb** (the action)

   They can have other parts as well, such as:
   - **an object** (the person or thing acted upon)
   - **a complement** (additional information about the subject)
   - **adverbials** (additional information about the verb)

   When they form part of other sentences, simple sentences are usually referred to as **clauses**.

2. **Compound sentences join two or more sentences together**. The two parts are joined by **coordinating conjunctions**, such as 'and', 'but' or 'or'. For example: Do you want to catch the bus or will you walk home?

3. **Complex sentences** have **two or more clauses joined by subordinating conjunctions**, such as 'although', 'because' or 'if'. The **main clause** makes sense on its own. The **subordinate clause** does not make sense on its own; for example:

   > I didn't see you at the party **although** I looked everywhere.

   > **If** you read in this light, you'll hurt your eyes.

4. **Minor sentences** usually consist of a single verb or verb phrase. They are often used in instructions or commands, for example: Listen.

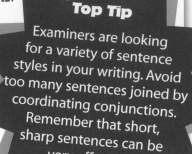

Top Tip
Examiners are looking for a variety of sentence styles in your writing. Avoid too many sentences joined by coordinating conjunctions. Remember that short, sharp sentences can be very effective.

Note that the subordinate clause can occur at the beginning of the sentence as well as at the end.

The anatomy of a sentence

The **different parts of speech**, such as **noun**, **pronoun**, **adjective**, **verb** and **adverb**, **conjunctions** and **prepositions**, can be single words or short phrases:

-
  adjective · noun · verb · adverb
  Old   Alex   walked   slowly.

- Last Wednesday   the   early   train   was derailed,   unexpectedly.
  adverbial phrase · *adjective* · *noun* · *verb* · *adverb*

It is important to remember that you can only tell what part of speech a word or phrase is when it is in a sentence. For example:

> *London* looks like a noun because it is the name of a place, but in the sentence *I caught the London bus* it is an adjective.

> *Walk* looks like a verb because it is an action, but in the sentence *They went for a walk* it is a noun.

Variety within sentences

As well as using all the different sentence types, you will impress examiners if you **vary the internal structure of your sentences**. Two ways of doing this involve:

- placing the most important information at the beginning of the sentence
- withholding important information until the end to create suspense.

For example: *Passing my driving test was probably one of the proudest moments of my life* places emphasis on the passing of the test; whereas *One of the proudest moments of my life was probably passing my driving test* uses exactly the same words but places the emphasis on how the speaker felt.

The passive voice

The **passive voice places emphasis on the thing done rather than the person or thing performing an action**. It uses part of the verb *to be*, such as *is* or *was*, plus a past participle, such as *heard* or *taken*. For example:

- Two pills are to be taken twice per day.
- The glass was broken.

However, **overuse of the passive should be avoided**. Writing is rather flat if you don't know who is doing what.

The use of pronouns

Pronouns stand in for nouns, e.g. I, you, he, she, it, we, they, him, her, its, himself. In a compound sentence it often makes sense not to repeat the noun. However, if there is more than one character involved, **pronouns can become confusing**. Can you understand the following sentence?

> Patrick gave the CD to Joe but he was annoyed when he didn't tell him that he had recorded it.

Its and it's

Its is a possessive pronoun which causes problems because of its similarity to *it's* – the short form of *it is*, e.g. *It's annoying when the dog loses its bone.*

If you can't decide which version you should use, try expanding the short form to its longer form, e.g. **It is** *annoying when the dog loses* **it is** *bone*. The first it's makes sense but the second one doesn't.

Quick Test

True or false?

1. Independent clauses can make sense on their own.

2. 'When you look into them' is a sentence.

3. The sentence, 'Write your name in block capitals' is a statement.

4. Varying your sentences can improve your expression.

Answers 1. True. 2. False. 3. False: it is a command or an instruction. 4. True.

Spellings

Methods of learning tricky spellings

1. Look up words in **dictionaries** and check their spellings. Dictionaries work on the alphabet principle for each word and finding words becomes easier with practice. Carry a small dictionary with you. Relying on teachers and others to spell words for you means that you will never really learn them. Aim to be an independent learner.

2. The **Look–Say–Cover–Write–Check** method is successful as long as you have spelled the word correctly in the first place. Learning words by repeating this process does work.

3. Try writing a crazy but **memorable sentence** using each letter of the word (a **mnemonic**). For example, a mnemonic for the word believe could be: *Big Elephants Look Inside Elephantine Vases Everywhere*. However, only use this method for the few words that are the biggest problems for you, otherwise you will have too many strange phrases to remember.

4. Use the **sound of words** to help you spell them. Work your way through each syllable as you aim to spell the word. This works for many words and is always worth trying before using other methods.

5. For **tricky plural endings**:
   - If a noun ends with a 'y' and it has a letter such as 't', 'r' or 'n' before the 'y', you need to add 'ies' to the plural. For example: **diary – diaries**; **curry – curries**; **company – companies**; **city – cities**.
   - If the last letter before the 'y' is a vowel (a, e, i, o, u) you have to add an 's' to make the plural. For example: **boy – boys**; **journey – journeys**; **key – keys**; **guy – guys**; **monkey – monkeys**.
   - Words which end in 'fe', such as *knife*, take 'ves' in plurals; similarly, words ending in 'f', like *shelf* or *half*, change to *shelves* and *halves* in plurals.

6. Use **'i' before 'e' except after 'c'**; for example; *thief* and *sieve*, but *receive*.

7. **Proof-read** your work for words that you are likely to spell incorrectly. Make a list of these words from a number of subjects and focus on learning them.

Word families

A good way of improving your spelling is to realise that words belong to **word families**. This means that, if you know the basic word, you will have a good idea about other similar words. For instance, the spelling of *criticism* is easier if you remember that it is related to *critic*. Here are some other useful word families.

- **act**, actor, action, activity, react, reaction
- **assist**, assistant, assistance
- **balance**, imbalance, unbalanced
- **bore**, boring, boredom
- **call**, recall, calling
- **child**, children, childhood, childlike, childish, childless
- **claim**, reclaim, reclamation, disclaim
- **cover**, discover, discovery, uncover
- **critic**, criticism, criticise, critique
- **electric**, electrical, electricity, electrician, electronic, electrocute
- **examine**, examination, examiner, examinee
- **fill**, fulfil, fulfilling, fulfilment
- **give**, given, forgive, forgiveness
- **govern**, governor, government
- **hand**, handler, handy, handicraft
- **hero**, heroic, heroism
- **joy**, joyful, enjoy, enjoyment
- **light**, lightening, lightning, delighted, enlighten
- **machine**, machinery, machinist
- **medic**, medical, medication
- **native**, nation, national, nativity
- **nature**, natural, unnatural, denatured
- **obey**, disobey, disobedient
- **operate**, operator, cooperate, cooperation
- **pack**, packet, package
- **pain**, painkiller, painful, painless, painstaking
- **pass**, passage, passenger
- **press**, impress, depression, repress, express
- **prison**, imprison, imprisonment
- **prove**, approval, disapprove
- **public**, publication, publicity, publicise
- **relate**, relative, relation
- **shake**, shakily, shaken
- **sign**, signatory, signature, signal, resign, resignation
- **sum**, summary, summation, assume, assumption
- **syllable**, monosyllable, monosyllabic, polysyllabic
- **take**, mistake, mistaken, overtaken, overtaking, partaking.

Quick Test

1. What is the difference between an *examiner* and an *examinee*?
2. Can you think of any other words that make this distinction?
3. What connection can you see between the meanings of the words *operate* and *cooperation*?
4. Can you explain why *fulfil* and *fulfilment* are spelled differently from *fulfilling*?

Answers 1. An *examiner* is the person doing the examining; an *examinee* is the person being examined. **2.** Nominator, nominee; payer, payee; trainer, trainee. The other half of the pair for words like *refugee* and *evacuee* is not used. **3.** They both have to do with work. **4.** The 'l' is doubled in *fulfilling* to keep the 'i' sound short.

Words often misspelled

Commonly misspelled words

A–F

accommodation
actually
alcohol
although
analyse
analysis
argument
assessment
atmosphere
audible
audience
autumn

beautiful
beginning
believe
beneath
buried
business

caught
chocolate
climb
column
concentration
conclusion
conscience
consequence
continuous
creation

daughter
decide
decision
definite
design
development
diamond
diary
disappear
disappoint

embarrass
energy
engagement
enquire
environment
evaluation
evidence
explanation

February
fierce
forty
fulfil
furthermore

G–O

guard

happened
health
height

imaginary
improvise
industrial
interesting
interrupt
issue

jealous

knowledge

listening
lonely
lovely

marriage
material
meanwhile
miscellaneous
mischief
modern
moreover
murmur

necessary
nervous

original
outrageous

P–R

parallel
participation
pattern
peaceful
people
performance
permanent
persuade
persuasion
physical
possession
potential
preparation
prioritise
proportion
proposition

questionnaire
queue

reaction
receive
reference
relief
research
resources

S–W

safety
Saturday
secondary
separate
sequence
shoulder
sincerely
skilful
soldier
stomach
straight
strategy
strength
success
surely
surprise

technique
technology
tomorrow

unfortunately

Wednesday
weight
weird
women

Top Tip

English is a notoriously difficult language to spell; however, with effort you can overcome most obvious misspellings. Why not go through the lists here and try some of the exercises suggested on page 16? The main learning method is: Look–Say–Cover–Write–Check.

Common homophones and confusions

Homophones sound the same, but have different meanings.

a lot, allot (*never alot as a single word*)

advise, advice (*verb, noun*)

affect, effect (*to influence, a result*)

allowed, aloud (*permitted, out loud*)

bean, been (*as in baked bean, part of the verb to be*)

beech, beach (*tree, seashore*)

blue, blew (*colour, air moved*)

board, bored (*wood or group of managers, uninterested*)

bought, brought (*purchased, carried*)

break, brake (*damage, slow down*)

by, buy, bye (*next to or responsible for, purchase, farewell*)

cell, sell (*enclosed space, dispose of for money*)

cent, scent, sent (*coin, smell, dispatched*)

cereal, serial (*grain, a story in parts*)

choose, chose (*present tense, past tense*)

cloth, clothe (*material, to dress*)

conscience, conscious (*sense of right or wrong, aware*)

course, coarse (*route or direction, rough*)

dear, deer (*beloved or expensive, animal*)

fate, fete (*destiny, celebration*)

flour, flower (*bread ingredient, part of plant*)

grate, great (*metal grid, very large*)

hair, hare (*on head, animal*)

herd, heard (*group, listened to*)

here, hear (*this place, listen*)

him, hymn (*that man, religious song*)

hole, whole (*pit, complete*)

hour, our (*time, belonging to us*)

it's, its (*it is, belonging to it*)

key, quay (*lock opener, boat dock*)

knight, night (*wears armour, darkness*)

knot, not (*rope tie or nautical speed, negative*)

know, no (*be aware, negative*)

made, maid (*built or done, servant*)

main, mane (*important, lion's hair*)

meet, meat (*come together, animal flesh*)

might, mite (*may or strength, small insect or small amount*)

morning, mourning (*early part of day, grieving*)

new, knew (*recent, was aware*)

pane, pain (*part of window, hurt*)

peace, piece (*quiet, segment or part*)

place, plaice (*location, fish*)

plane, plain (*flat surface or short for aeroplane, not beautiful or large expanse of flat land*)

practise, practice (*to practise, a practice*)

quiet, quite (*not loud, fairly*)

read, reed (*e.g. read a book, kind of grass*)

rein, rain, reign (*horse equipment, water, royal rule*)

right, write (*correct, use pen*)

rode, road, rowed (*used vehicle, carriageway, used oars*)

scene, seen (*part of play, looked at*)

see, sea (*look, body of water*)

sew, so, sow (*use needle and thread, therefore, plant seed*)

site, sight (*place, vision*)

source, sauce (*origin, food supplement*)

stair, stare (*steps, look hard*)

steel, steal (*metal, take*)

sum, some (*total, a few*)

sun, son (*thing in sky, male descendant*)

tail, tale (*part of animal, story*)

their, they're, there (*belonging to them, they are, that place*)

too, two, to (*in addition, 2, in the direction of*)

vain, vein (*self admiring, blood vessel*)

waist, waste (*below stomach, not used*)

week, weak (*seven days, without strength*)

where, wear (*which place, clothes*)

you, yew, ewe (*person, tree, female sheep*)

you're, your (*you are, belonging to you*)

Synonyms

Synonyms are words that have similar meanings, for example:

- beautiful – pretty, nice, fine, good-looking, elegant, lovely, fair
- display – show, exhibit, exhibition, spread, open, expose, demonstration, layout.

Structures

Connective words link phrases, sentences and paragraphs together.

Top Tip
The skilful use of **connectives** can help you to vary your sentence structure and improve your style.

Ordering your ideas

Words that help to put your ideas in order
- *firstly, then, so far, secondly, in the end, next, eventually, subsequently, at last, at length, afterwards*

Words for exceptions
- *only, if, unless, except (for), save for*

Making points and giving examples

Words used to argue and make points
- *consequently, thus, so, as a result, because, as, hence, therefore, since, until, whenever, accordingly, as long as*

Words to help you give examples
- *for example, for instance, such as, take the case of, thus, as (evidence), to show that, as revealed by*

Words for extra points or ideas
- *and, too, what is more, also, furthermore, and then, again, moreover, as well as, in addition*

Words to emphasise points
- *above all, in particular, notably, specifically, indeed, more important, especially, significant(ly), in fact*

> in addition
> take the case of
> as a result
> above all
> therefore

Paragraphing

Paragraphs are necessary to break the text flow and help the reader to follow the writer's meaning.

- Paragraphs are **groups of sentences connected by the same topic**. Each paragraph carries a main idea.
- The main sentence of a paragraph is often found at the beginning and it is called a **topic sentence**. For example: *Successful students plan their revision in each subject. They plan how much time they have available and then try to cover a number of areas in each subject.*
- Any paragraphs following the first paragraph will need to **begin on a new line, indented 2 cm from the page margin**.
- You can link your paragraphs together skilfully by using the **connecting words** found in the boxes on these pages.

Being persuasive and analytical

Words to persuade

- *of course, naturally, obviously, clearly, certainly, surely, evidently*

Words to help you show an opinion or analyse

- *it would seem, to suggest, one might conclude / propose / deduce / infer / imply / say / consider*

Comparing and contrasting

Words to make a contrast or show what is different

- *but, nevertheless, alternatively, despite this, on the contrary, however, yet, the opposite, instead, whereas, to turn to, although, still, on the other hand*

Words to compare things in your writing or show what is similar

- *equally, in the same way, as with, likewise, similarly, compared with, an equivalent*

Essay endings

Words to sum up or end with

- *in brief, in summary, throughout, in all, on the whole, to sum up, overall, finally, to conclude, to recap, in the end*

in summary
on the whole
to conclude

Top Tip

Use appropriate and varied connective words in your essays to signpost your arguments.

Quick Test

1. Why use paragraphs?

2. Identify two words that can help you to compare pieces of writing.

3. What is the difference between *comparing* and *contrasting*?

4. Give two words that help to emphasise points in writing.

5. What do the words *furthermore* and *moreover* help you to do?

Answers 1. Paragraphs help readers to follow your ideas. They also break up the text according to topics. **2.** Any of the following: *in the same way, similarly, equally, as with, likewise, compared with, an equivalent*. **3.** To compare is to look for similarities and to contrast is to look for differences. **4.** Any of the following: *indeed, in particular, above all, notably, specifically, more importantly, especially, significantly,* in fact. **5.** They help you to make extra points or ideas.

Improve your style

Control

Teachers and examiners are looking for control in your writing. This means an awareness of the effect that **different writing techniques** can have and **deliberate use of them**.

Vocabulary and choice of words

The words you choose need to be **appropriate** for the task and as **accurate** as possible. For example, does your character get into a car, a battered old Ford, a people carrier or an oversized all-terrain vehicle? Do characters 'say' things all the time or do they 'mutter', 'mumble' or 'shout'?

Varying sentences and paragraphs

You already know about using different types of sentences, but you should also think about the **rhythm of your writing**. Large stretches of **long sentences can create a sense of continuity and flow**, but they can also become monotonous.
Try short sentences for emphasis. Even more emphatic than the short sentence is the short paragraph.

A single sentence paragraph really stands out.

You can build up tension by using short, snappy sentences that make the reader pause over each detail:

> 'I ran. Ran for all I was worth! Sometimes I stumbled over tree roots. Branches slashed my face. Something was rapidly hunting me down. Twigs and branches snapped in the desperate rushing behind me. A savage, wolf-like howl tore the air. Something clasped my leg! "God help me!" I screamed, as I gasped for breath.'

Varying sentence structures

The first part of a sentence tends to contain the subject. In the middle of the sentence there is often known information – the new information comes at the end. From time to time you can vary this order. Compare the impact of: *As I put the car into gear the engine went 'thunk'* with *'Thunk' went the engine as I put the car into gear*.

You also have a great deal of choice when it comes to the placing of **adverbial phrases**. These tell you about things like time, mood and manner. For example:

- *With deliberate slowness,* Dr Shrike marked out the area he was going to cut.
- Dr Shrike, *with deliberate slowness,* marked out the area he was going to cut.
- Dr Shrike marked out the area he was going to cut *with deliberate slowness.*

Descriptive writing

The power of descriptive writing comes in the **accurate choice of nouns and verbs**. Adjectives and adverbs can help to pin down what you say even more accurately. Always make sure that your adjectives or adverbs are doing some work. For example, *he walked slowly* could be conveyed with the single verb *he strolled*; *a gnarled oak* will create a much clearer picture in your readers' minds than *a big twisted tree*. Finally, remember to **appeal to all five senses in descriptive writing**.

Some pitfalls to avoid

- Do not confuse big words with a sophisticated style. Remember that you want to give your readers as clear a picture as possible.
- Do not overdo any one effect. If all your sentences have an unusual structure, people will find it distracting.
- Use figurative language sparingly. One well-chosen simile or metaphor will stand out like a rose in a desert.

Top Tip

A clear, fluent, written style is something that you are going to have to work at. Examine the style of the writers you are studying and think about phrases, words and punctuation that could work for you.

How to improve your expression

Clarity and brevity

- Keep what you write **brief**, **simple** and **clear**.
- **Avoid long-winded, pompous sentences**; for example: *I remained in my abode and passed the time watching uninteresting programmes while looking at the little box in the corner.* This is tedious; try this instead: *I stayed at home watching boring programmes on TV.*

Clichés

Clichés are **tired expressions and imagery** that have **lost impact because of overuse**. Avoid the following:

like the plague   *like two ships that pass in the night*
food for thought   *leaves much to be desired*

Writing effective sentences

In a stylish, effective sentence:

- the beginning is the second-most important part;
- the middle is the least important part;
- the end is the most important part.

Take, for example, this line from Shakespeare's *Twelfth Night*:
'Some are born great, some achieve greatness and some have greatness thrust upon 'em.'

Avoid overworked words because they can be boring and repetitive, e.g. got, get, nice, good, totally, a lot of, kind of.

Avoid using tautologies – that is, repeating yourself unnecessarily, e.g. final end, sad misfortune, puzzling mystery.

Also try to **avoid reinforcing words** with words that would be better left out; your writing will have more impact without them. Word-reinforcement to avoid includes: totally wrong, absolutely fantastic, seriously consider.

Circumlocutions

Circumlocutions are **roundabout ways of saying things**. Again, stick to simple words or expressions, as these are usually more effective:

- in a majority of cases = usually
- in the event that = if
- owing to the fact that = because

- in less than no time = quickly
- on the grounds that = because
- with the exception of = except.

Top Tip

Try to improve your expression as you develop the habit of proof-reading your work. The Russian writer Chekhov said, 'Rewrite everything five times!'

Quick Test

1. Reduce these phrases to one word:
   a) due to the fact that
   b) pink in colour
   c) in this day and age.

2. What is the danger of overdoing description?

3. Identify a cliché and explain why you should try to avoid clichés in your writing.

Test your progress

Use the questions to test your progress.
Check your answers at the back of the book on page 94–5.

Punctuation and sentences

1. Try to sum up in a sentence why you need to punctuate your writing.

   ....

2. Identify five instances where you would need a capital letter.

   ....

3. Correct the following sentences by putting in capital letters where they are necessary:

   • jemma read Great Expectations for her english coursework. she had never read charles dickens before; she may read another one of his novels before easter.

   ....

4. Identify four of the five punctuation marks that can complete a sentence.

   ....

5. Explain one of the uses that semi-colons can serve.

   ....

6. What is a rhetorical question?

   ....

7. Identify one use for colons.

   ....

8. Give three of the four rules of direct speech.

   ....

9. What are the two main purposes of apostrophes?

   ....

10. Where does the apostrophe need to go with plural nouns that do not need an 's' to make them plurals?

    ....

11. Identify three of the four types of sentences grouped according to what they do.

    ....

12. Point out the main and dependent clauses of this sentence:

    • I will go to see the new movie at the cinema as soon as I have done the washing up.

    ....

Spelling and expression

13. Point out two methods of learning tricky spellings.

    ....

14. What is before 'e' except after 'c'?

....

15. Why do the following plurals end in 'ies': twenties, lorries, cities, injuries and berries?

....

16. Why do the following plurals end in 's': journeys, trolleys, donkeys, chimneys, toys?

....

17. What do 'here', 'there' and 'where' have in common?

....

18. Correct the following spellings: begginning, apperance, intrested, grammer, tonge, definately, neccesity, rythm, sentance.

....

19. What are synonyms?

....

20. Why are homophones confusing?

....

21. What are connectives?

....

22. What is the purpose of connectives in writing?

....

23. Why is it necessary to use paragraphs?

....

24. What is a topic sentence?

....

25. Briefly explain what 'control' means in writing.

....

26. Reduce this circumlocution to one word: 'on the grounds that'.

....

27. The following piece of writing has ten errors involving punctuation. Write it out correctly.

The opening line of Tennysons poem the eagle is very striking.
    'He clasps the crag with crooked hands'
The most noticeable thing about it is the use of the word hands where the reader might have expected something like talons or claws. The second thing that makes the line striking is the alliteration on the letter c. The repeated cs give the line a harsh sound which is in keeping with the eagles harsh environment.

How did you do?

1–9	correct	....	start again
10–15	correct	....	getting there
16–22	correct	....	good work
23–27	correct	....	excellent

Transactional writing

What you are expected to do

The task for your W1 folio piece is to **produce a piece of writing that either conveys information or deploys ideas, expounds, argues and evaluates**. (You may choose to tackle another piece of writing like this in your exam.)

What you can write about

A transactional piece, W1, could be:

- an informative piece on a topic that interests you
- a piece of writing in which you give your view on a subject, for example, animal experimentation
- a discursive essay exploring two sides of a topic.

How you will be graded

To achieve Grades 1–3 you will need to:

- **research** your chosen topic carefully and then **use ideas and evidence** effectively
- **organise** your writing so that it is a detailed response to the task, with significant points being highlighted
- **interest** your readers and sustain points
- use an **appropriate** range of **punctuation** to make your meaning clear
- use **your own words**
- show both **elaboration** and **conciseness** in your writing
- use **wide-ranging vocabulary** in which syntax, spelling and punctuation is **accurate** and **varied**
- consciously use language to achieve sophisticated effects
- produce a **well-structured** piece of work
- write between 600–800 words.

Top Tip

Always consider the purpose and intended audience of your writing.

Top Tip

Develop your paragraphs in a variety of ways: provide evidence, give examples, use statistics, compare and contrast, illustrate with anecdote, question and answer. Remember that good paragraphs have effective topic sentences.

Organising transactional writing

Consider the **task and topic**, and think about the **appropriate form of writing**: an article, essay, letter, etc. Topics that would meet the requirement for a W1 piece might include:

- an informative piece on an activity you are involved in
- a biography of someone in your family
- your viewpoint on a controversial area, such as the use of CCTV and issues of privacy.

Researching your topic

Once you have chosen a topic, do the **research**: see experts who know the topic, go to libraries, use the Internet, look in encyclopedias, write to associated organisations.

Make notes on one side of a piece of paper; number any pages that you use. Alternatively, make a mind-map if you prefer. Instructions on how to produce a mind-map are given on pages 38–41.

Planning your writing

Once you have completed your notes, look over them and **plan your piece of writing** on a single sheet of paper. Number your points; this could be organised as a brainstorm.

Drafting your essay

Remember to **write your title** when you write or type your first draft. If you hand-write your work, leave every second line blank for proof-reading and alterations; this will make it easier to check your work at each draft. **Always proof-read your work for spelling, punctuation and expression**. Remember to proof-read your final draft again for the errors that you are likely to make.

A plan for a discursive essay

Introduction – Introduce the topic and state your attitude clearly.

Paragraph 2 – Introduce your first point in support of your viewpoint.

Paragraph 3 – Make a second point in support and develop your stance.

Paragraph 4 – Produce a final argument in support of your view.

Paragraph 5 – State an opposite view and then refute it.

Paragraph 6 – Conclude with a strong re-statement of your view and a summation of your key points.

Top Tip

Always produce at least two drafts of your work. Your second draft should be your best one.

Quick Test

1. What is it that you are doing when you look over your work again?

2. How many drafts should you make of your work?

3. Identify three places where you could find information for your chosen topic.

Answers 1. Proof-reading. 2. At least two. 3. Libraries, encyclopedias, the Internet, knowledgeable people, associated organisations.

Expressive writing

Describing personal experience

What you are expected to do

A personal experience essay is one of the options for your second, W2, folio piece. Your task is to write an essay in which you not only **describe a personal experience** but, more importantly, **express your thoughts and feelings**, and **reflect upon the event** detailed in your writing.

It is crucial that your essay does not simply re-tell a story. The marker will be looking for evidence of **how the experience has affected you** and will expect to see aspects of your personality shine through the words you use. You should therefore attempt to **write sensitively about yourself** and **be genuine in your thoughts, feelings and reactions**.

Good essays will **reveal insights gained by the writer** as a result of the experience being described and **show a high degree of self-awareness**. Your sense of involvement will be clear from your writing.

How you will be graded

As well as the key issues of accurate punctuation and effective paragraphing, a good personal experience essay will:

provide a concise account of the event with a clear sense of involvement

be well sustained

demonstrate a degree of insight

have some style to it

show self-awareness

express your personal feelings and reactions with a degree of sensitivity

What you can write about

There is no set task for your folio work, so **the choice is yours**. In the exam you may be offered an assignment which lets you write a personal experience style essay, and in such a situation it would be important to stick to the task.

Pupils often choose to write about **an event that they remember vividly**, either because it was a particularly exhilarating time, such as a public performance, or because it was an extremely emotional time, such as a family bereavement. However, **be careful not to overdo any sense of emotion** – good or bad – as this can lead to quite clichéd writing.

Top Tip

Be genuine in a personal essay. Markers can almost always spot when a student has invented an experience.

Planning

As with all writing, your essay will benefit from some **pre-writing planning**. An important feature that markers look for is **structure**. This can be difficult to achieve if you do not prepare properly.

Time spent on preparation is time well spent!

Begin by creating a title that sets out your task. It does not have to be clever or intriguing: the title is not part of your essay but part of your planning! Once you have your 'working title', brainstorm some ideas around it; you could use a spidergram. From here you can begin to structure your essay into clear paragraphs.

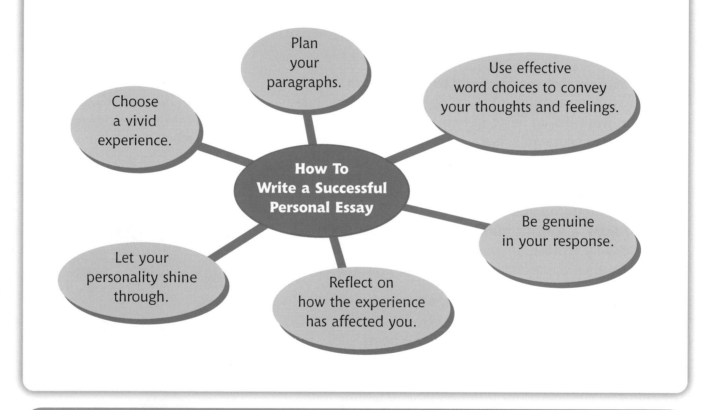

Plan your paragraphs.

Use effective word choices to convey your thoughts and feelings.

Choose a vivid experience.

How To Write a Successful Personal Essay

Be genuine in your response.

Let your personality shine through.

Reflect on how the experience has affected you.

Quick Test

1. A personal experience essay is a work of fiction. True or False?

2. Clichéd writing means
   a) writing that is fresh and original
   b) writing that uses worn out phrases and predictable events
   c) writing that has a twist in the tale

3. 'Insight' means a) self awareness or b) good vision.

4. What is the best way to ensure a sense of structure to your essay?

5. What is the best way to convey thoughts and feelings?

Answers 1. False. **2.** (b.) **3.** (a) **4.** Planning. **5.** Effective word choice.

Creative writing

What you are expected to do

A second option for your W2 piece is to produce a creative piece of writing in a **specific literary genre**, the most popular of which is the short story.

- In this task you will be **assessed on the quality of your writing**.

- There is **a wide range of possibilities regarding what you may write about** because there are no restrictions on form, content or genre. The key requirement is that the piece should be broadly expressive in nature. For example, a letter of complaint to your local council would not meet this requirement (although it could be a W1 piece); however, an imaginary letter home from a soldier suffering in the trenches would be acceptable.

- **Dramascripts** and **poetry** are acceptable forms for this assignment, but you would be well advised to check with your teacher before considering either of these options.

- **The SQA do not specify any particular length** for your work in terms of words or pages. The general rule is that work should be of an appropriate length for the task. As a general rule, however, around 800 words should be sufficient for a story; obviously you would use fewer words for poetry.

- What is most important is that the written piece has **clear aims**, a **specific purpose**, and that it is **effectively written**. If your work is **convincing and concise** then the examiner will give it a high grade.

- **Imaginative responses to literature** are also permissible, but again be advised by your teacher in this area. Writing the next chapter to a novel – for example, what happens to George from John Steinbeck's *Of Mice and Men* – is the type of work that could be considered for inclusion in your writing folio. However, it would be assessed as a piece of original writing not as a critical response to the text.

> Remember that you can word-process your work, which makes re-drafting much easier.

Internet

Go to the Learning Lab at www.leckieandleckie.co.uk for links to examples of excellent short stories.

What you can write about

Here are a few suggestions that you could choose from for a fictional piece of writing:

| write the opening of a novel, introducing the key character | keep an imaginary diary | write a one-act play | write a short horror story with a 'twist in the tale' |

Here are a few short story titles to get you going if you are stuck for ideas:

- 'My Last Day on Earth'
- 'Danger in Venice'
- 'Strange Meeting'
- 'The Visitors'
- 'Emergency on Alpha Minor'
- 'A Day in My Life as a Dog'

How you will be graded

To achieve Grades 1–3, you will need to:

write in the appropriate manner for the genre and purpose selected

use a varied range of sentences and vocabulary to keep your audience's interest

keep punctuation accurate and produce logical paragraphs to make your meaning clear

develop characters and settings within your narrative

use literary devices such as similes and metaphors effectively

write with flair and originality

show assured control in your writing, with a wide range of expression to achieve effects

show an awareness of tone in words and sentences

use the conventions of your selected genre effectively

be accurate in punctuation and spelling

Internet

If you would like to read an excellent story with an ingenious ending, read Liam O'Flaherty's The Sniper. *You can find the link in the Learning Lab.*
This story has a very short timeframe: its action takes place over a few hours. You could do the same in your story by writing about a single incident or an episode that lasts for only a few hours.

Quick Test

1. Which of the following would not be accepted as a 'specific literary genre'?
   a) Short story
   b) Discursive essay
   c) Poem
   d) Diary entry

2. What is the term for checking over your work and making corrections?

3. Using a variety of sentence structures will help do what?

4. Short stories may only be written in the folio. True or False?

5. Re-drafting work is made easier by using what tool?

Answers 1. (b) 2. Proof-reading. 3. Keep your reader interested. 4. False. 5. Word processing.

Writing short stories

Planning

Brainstorm or create a **spidergram** (or **mind-map**) of your ideas on a blank sheet of paper. Sometimes stories can come from a character; sometimes they can come from a specific situation such as a shipwreck or a sudden discovery. Once you have a few ideas, try to think of a title because this may help you to focus on the plot and characterisation of your story.

The **plot** is the plan or outline of your story.

- What will be the climax of your plot when your story reaches a crisis?
- What will be the result of the climax?
- From whose point of view is the story going to be told?

Style of narration

Decide if the style of narration is to be in the first or third person. A **first-person narrator** tells the story from within the story; a **third-person narrator** stands outside the story. How much will your narrator know and see? Will the third-person narrator be able to know everything that the characters are thinking? These are matters of **perspective**. Will the narrator be biased or objective in their viewpoint?

Top Tip

Try to use a few **literary devices**, such as similes, metaphors and alliteration, to create effects in your writing.

Characters

You will need a main character and two or three other important characters. You could include some minor ones, too. Create a brief **profile for each character** because this will enable you to be realistic in your portrayal of them. Have a checklist for each character, covering, for example, age, appearance, habits, job, traits, ambitions, hobbies, likes and dislikes, motivation, etc.

Setting

Where is the story going to be set?

- Will it be set at **home or abroad**?
- Is the story going to be set in the **present, future or past**?
- Will your story be **drawn from everyday life**?
- Perhaps you would prefer a fairy-tale setting **drawn from your imagination**?

How are you going to **describe the setting**? Will you suggest the setting through minor details in your writing, or will you be more elaborate in the details you give to describe the setting? If necessary, do a little research to make your setting convincing.

Genre

Choose a genre for your story. Is your story going to be:

an adventure?   a comedy?   a detective mystery?

science-fiction?   a romance?

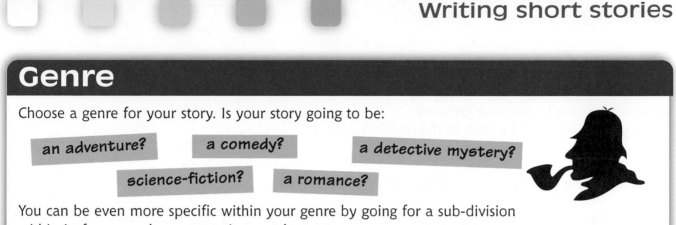

You can be even more specific within your genre by going for a sub-division within it, for example, a romantic comedy.

Structure

Ensure that you have a clear beginning, middle and end in your story.

You need to bait your story with a good 'hook' at the beginning, to make your readers want to read on.

> You could begin in the middle of **an exciting incident.**

> If your story involves suspense, try to include 'a twist in the tale'. Alternatively, you could give a moral to your story.

> You could use an **unusual** description or start from an unusual perspective, to **intrigue** the reader.

Look at examples in the stories you read.

Use of time

How are you going to tell your story? Will you tell your story in a **linear** (straightforward) way or through **flashbacks**? The plots of most stories, novels and plays are written in a linear manner, i.e. the plots and characters move forward naturally in time. In contrast, a novel such as *Wuthering Heights* (1847) by Emily Brontë moves forwards and backwards in time as various first-person narrators relate significant events in the novel.

Top Tip

The last part of your sentence usually carries the most impact, so recast your sentences to maximise your impact.

Quick Test

1. How is a first-person narrative told?

2. What does the term 'genre' mean?

3. What do you need at the beginning of a story to keep your readers interested in reading further?

4. What does it mean to 'elaborate'?

5. How can you make your characters believable?

Test your progress

Use the questions to test your progress.
Check your answers at the back of the book on page 95.

Writing

1. How many writing pieces contribute to your folio grade?

....

2. What is the word length that you should be aiming for?

....

3. What does 'transactional' mean?

....

4. What does 'expressive' mean?

....

5. What does 'imaginative' mean?

....

6. Give two examples of what you could write about as a W1 piece.

....

7. Give two examples of what you could write about as W2 piece.

....

8. Why is it important to express your thoughts and feelings in a personal experience type essay?

....

9. What does 'insight' mean?

....

10. What danger lies in being over emotional in your writing?

....

11. Why should you use a genuine experience in a personal experience essay?

....

12. Indicate two ways that paragraphs can be developed.

....

....

13. Similes are comparisons. How do they differ from metaphors?

....

14. Why should you use figurative language in your work?

....

15. What does 'hook' mean in terms of stories?

....

16. What is meant by 'setting'?

....

17. What are the main styles of narration?

....

18. If a narrator is outside the story, what is he or she?

....

19. What does 'plot' mean?

....

20. Give a method by which you can plan your story.

....

21. Explain what is meant by 'control' in writing.

....

22. If writing is 'linear', what is it?

....

23. If your task is 'discursive', how is it written?

....

24. Give three sources where you could find information on a topic.

....

25. Will an imaginative story be suitable for a W1 piece?

....

26. Other than short story, name two genres that would be acceptable as a specific literary form.

....

27. Are you allowed to word process your folio pieces?

....

28. What does 'proof-read' mean?

....

29. Other than the folio, where else are your writing skills assessed?

....

How did you do?

1–9	correct	start again
10–15	correct	getting there
16–22	correct	good work
23–29	correct	excellent

Critical essays

What is a critical essay?

Your ability to respond thoughtfully to literature is tested through the writing of **critical essays**. A critical essay is your written response to a text that you have studied, based on a set task. The 'text' may be a novel, a short story, poetry, a play or even a film. In the essay you **evaluate** the text and attempt to **demonstrate your understanding** of its main ideas and your **analysis** of the writer's technique and craft. You are also expected to reveal your **genuine personal reaction** to the text.

1: Planning

- Examine **key words** and **phrases** in the task to help you focus on your answer.
- **Brainstorm** an essay plan with your essay question in the middle of a blank piece of paper.
- Aim for **three or four main arguments** and group your points around them. Remember to include a note of any **sources used** and to acknowledge any **quotations**.

2: Writing an introduction

Sometimes it is hard to start essays. A good way to begin is to **answer the question briefly in the opening paragraph**. Look at your notes and mind-maps to help you.

The following example is of an opening paragraph for an essay question on *Educating Rita*. The question asks: *Re-read the early and last scenes of* Educating Rita. *Explain what Rita gains and loses in her determination to become educated.*

'*Educating Rita by Willy Russell tells the story of Rita White, a 26-year-old hairdresser, who is trying to "find herself". Rita's gains can be summed up as follows: …*'

3: The main body

Work through **each main argument** from your introduction as **fully** as you can. Once you think that you have proved an argument sufficiently, move on to your next argument. Do not hammer away at the same point for too long.

Remember that your technique must be **point**, **evidence** and **comment**:
- make a key point in your argument;
- support it with evidence from the text;
- and then comment on the matter.

Use a wide range of **connective words** to link your points and arguments together (see pages 20–21). These words will bring your essay together. The skilful use of connectives can help the **fluency of arguments** in essays and make them easier to read.

Top Tip

Get an idea of what good essays look like. Ask your teacher for good examples of work by former pupils.

4: Conclusions

Your essay needs to embody a sense of **finality**. This should be reflected in the tone of your conclusion:

- Conclude by **summing up your arguments and findings**.
- **Give your views** on the text(s) that you are writing about.
- It is important to **explain what you gained** from reading the text(s).

Types of response

Imaginative responses to literature

This is an option for your reading folio. It is important to remember that while you will need to display some skill in the form chosen – dramascript, extra chapter, letter, report, etc. – the piece of work is still essentially a response to the text read. Your work will need to **demonstrate a thorough familiarity with the original text** through appropriate references and allusions, and you will need to be **sensitive to the mood and tone** of the original piece.

Media and imaginative responses

Writing a critical evaluation of a media text requires the same approach as for a literary text, with a focus on the task set. It is especially important that you do not simply re-tell the story (narrative) of a film you have studied. Use of appropriate **critical terminology** is essential: for example, *mise en scène*, representation, editing, camera angles, lighting, sound, etc. You need to **prepare thoroughly** in order to tackle a **critical evaluation** of a media text.

The term 'text' can refer to any form of writing and you should refer to your books, stories or poems as texts in your writing. Films, for the purpose of the folio requirements, are referred to as media texts.

Quick Test

1. What should you focus on in essay questions?

2. What does 'text' mean?

3. How many main arguments should you aim for?

Answers 1. Understanding the whole question and paying attention to key words and phrases. **2.** Any book, play or poem in any genre. Also includes film. **3.** Three or four.

Mind-maps for essays

Re-read your text

Whether you are reading a play, poem, novel or short story, you must **re-read your text** for **a deeper understanding of your essay question or task**.

- When creating a task for a folio piece, many teachers concentrate on a **writer's technique** and how this **aids our understanding of the text**.

- For plays, teachers may focus on **conflict as a central issue** and ask you to examine how the writer develops this through **characterisation and plot**.

- For novels, you might be expected to show how a **theme, character, imagery** or **mood**, has been represented.

- For poetry, you will certainly be looking at **the poet's choice of words** and **use of imagery and figurative language**.

One of the best ways of making notes for your essay is to produce a memorable mind-map or spidergram.

When to use a spidergram/mind-map

If your essay title asks you to write about a character, theme or any aspect of a text that you are studying, you could do a mind-map like the one on the opposite page. **Study your essay question** and try to build up relevant comments by **looking carefully at key words and phrases in your question**. Check your ideas again by **re-reading key parts of the text**.

Study the characters

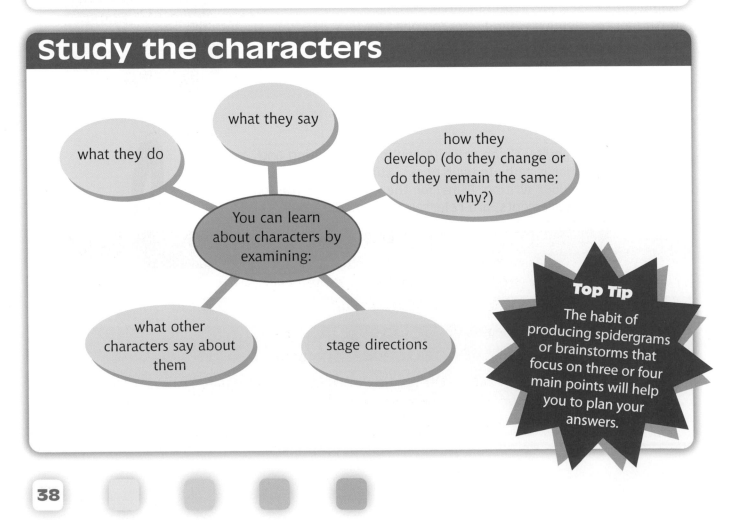

Top Tip

The habit of producing spidergrams or brainstorms that focus on three or four main points will help you to plan your answers.

Build your mind-map as you read

A mind-map for a character study

Go through the text and look at the places where your character speaks or others speak about him or her. Build your mind-map up gradually, as follows:

1. Use white paper without lines – it helps you think more clearly.

2. Use a pencil and a rubber – it is quicker and you can also add colours.

3. **Begin in the middle of the page** with a title (use the words of the task to create a suitable title) and put the most important information around the title.

4. Work your way out to the **margins**, where you should put **the least important information**.

5. Your **first five minutes** are likely to be the **most productive** so do not stop for anything. You can make your map pretty and memorable afterwards. Remember that the **colours** you choose for various topics of your mind-map can be meaningful because everything can be given an appropriate colour.

6. **Make connections between ideas by running branches off your main ideas**. Draw connecting branches to other main ideas if it seems sensible. It will then take on the character of a colourful tube map; you can then add appropriate pictures and images.

7. Keep mind-maps to one piece of paper. If you run out of space, tape another sheet of paper on to the side of the paper where you are running out of space. It does not matter how big your piece of paper is as long as your mind-map is on one side of paper. You can always carefully fold it up afterwards.

Top Tip

Try to get an overview of the themes of your particular play. Then see how a character relates to these themes.

Quick Test

1. What is gained by a re-reading of a text, before attempting a task?

2. How can you keep comments relevant to the task?

3. List three ways that we learn about characters.

4. Where should the title or topic of the mind-map be placed?

5. Why should you not stop during the first five minutes of brainstorming a mind-map?

Test your progress

Use the questions to test your progress.

Check your answers at the back of the book on page 94.

Question A

Choose just one answer: a, b, c, or d.

1. Which of the following is not suitable as a subject for a mind-map?

a) discussing a theme

b) exploring a character

c) telling the story of a play or novel

d) investigating imagery

2. Before you begin a mind-map, you should:

a) make sure you have suitable pens and paper available

b) check the key words of the question for suitable headings

c) brainstorm ideas

d) sharpen your pencils

3. What is the point in colouring in a completed mind-map?

a) it looks good.

b) the colour makes it easier to remember.

c) the different colours are a way of grouping ideas together.

d) to make it look like a map of the London tube

4. A mind-map is a good method of planning because:

a) it helps you see the connections between ideas

b) it makes a memorable revision aid

c) unexpected connections sometimes come up

d) it's a more creative approach than just jotting down points

Question B

Study the notes below on *Macbeth* and then complete the task that follows.

Question: 'Are the witches responsible for the tragedy of *Macbeth*?'

- Sailor speech shows that they can't directly change fate.
- Temptation – Use the truth against him, Thane of Cawdor greeting is true when they utter it.
- Temptation 2 – All three warnings are true. Just not what Macbeth expected.
- Effect on Macbeth – Witches not present at murder – his decision.
- Effect on Lady Macbeth – Letter describes meeting – she persuades Macbeth.
- Conclusion.

1. Rearrange these notes as a mind-map.

2. Which version is easier to follow?

Question C: Folio practice task

Planning an essay

Use a mind-map to plan an essay that discusses Shakespeare's presentation of the main character of the play you have studied. (If you haven't studied a play by Shakespeare, simply adjust the task to suit a play that you have read.)

Consider:

- How we are introduced to the character.
- How the character changes.
- Key relationships.
- Important plot developments.

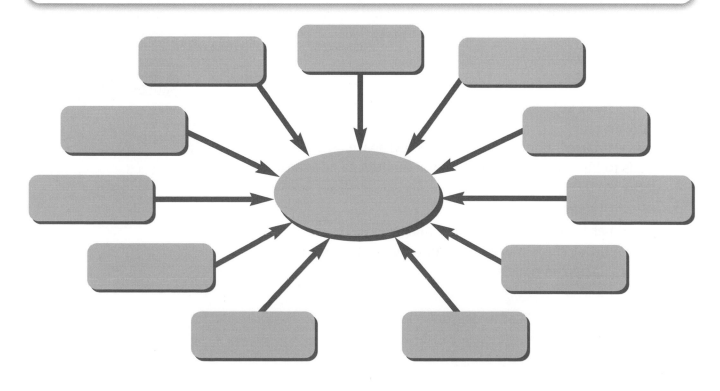

Studying prose

Novels and short stories (prose) are studied as part of the Standard Grade course.

How you will be graded

You will be assessed on your ability to show through your writing your understanding and appreciation of texts that you have read.

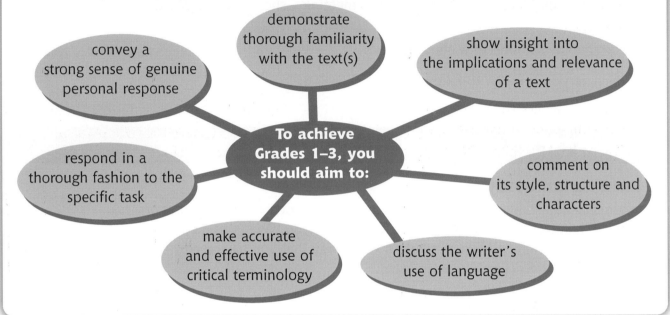

To achieve Grades 1–3, you should aim to:

- demonstrate thorough familiarity with the text(s)
- convey a strong sense of genuine personal response
- show insight into the implications and relevance of a text
- respond in a thorough fashion to the specific task
- comment on its style, structure and characters
- make accurate and effective use of critical terminology
- discuss the writer's use of language

Comparing novels and stories

Novels and stories have **plots** and **stories**, may include **dialogue**, have **characters** and set out **themes** and **ideas**.

Short stories differ from novels in that they:

- are usually based upon a specific incident or point in time
- usually have just one main plot and no space for sub-plots or sub-texts
- have less description because there is less space: any description needs to be economical and essential in order to add meaning to the story
- use striking details
- sometimes have more fragmented dialogue
- include fewer characters who do and say more in less space than characters in novels.

What to look for in characters

When you are studying the characters in your novel, you should look out for the following things.

- The **names of characters** sometimes tell you more about them. For example, Pip from *Great Expectations* is named after a seed. One of the novel's main themes is his development and growth as he changes from a lower-class boy to a gentleman. The novel charts the education of his heart as well as his mind.

- **Flat and round characters**. E.M. Forster created these terms to describe types of characters found in novels in his book *Aspects of the Novel* (1927). Flat characters do not develop in novels and are generally not as important as round characters, who develop because they change in the course of a novel. The same terms can be applied to characters in short stories.

- **How a character interacts with other characters** and **what other characters say about him or her**. This can help readers to understand other aspects of a character's personality.

- Any **direct comments** on the character by a **third-person narrator**.

- If the character that you are studying is the narrator of your story, **how far can you trust** what he or she says? Do they have **self-knowledge** or do they have a lot to learn? Could they be termed **an unreliable narrator**?

- What characters look like: the **physical appearance** of characters given in their description often tells us more about them.

- What a character **says and does**; much can be inferred from talk and action.

First- or third-person narrator

Do writers tell the story from the point of view of a character within the story as 'I' or 'me' – that is, as a first-person narrator? Or is the story told by a third-person narrator, who looks at what is going on from outside? The **writer's choice of who tells the story** can determine how we see, understand and interpret characters, as well as themes and ideas within a story.

First-person narrators usually have **a limited point of view**. They are so close to what is happening that they cannot see everything that is going on or know what other characters are thinking. Yet first-person narrators can **reveal much more of themselves**.

Third-person narrators can see and know much more. They can know everything if the writer wants them to. This last kind of narrator is called an **omniscient narrator**.

It is important to understand that whatever the first- or third-person narrator thinks is **not necessarily what the writer thinks**. Show in your writing that you understand that **writers adopt masks by using narrators** in their stories.

Top Tip

Always check to see if a story is written in the first or third person.

Quick Test

1. What does 'genre' mean?

2. What does 'prose' mean

3. What is a first-person narrative?

4. What is a third-person narrative?

Answers 1. 'Type' – as in romance, Western or detective fiction. **2.** Prose means ordinary language, and is used to describe written works such as novels, as opposed to poetry or verse. **3.** A first-person narrative is a story told through the eyes of one of its characters. **4.** A third-person narrative is a story that is told from the point of view of an outsider looking in.

Themes and mood

Themes

Themes are **ideas or messages that writers explore in their stories**. The novel is a form of writing that allows writers to examine more than one theme.

For example, in *Roll of Thunder Hear My Cry* (1976), Mildred D. Taylor explores the theme of **growing up** and the coming of age of its main character, Cassie Logan. She experiences **racism** in 1930s' Mississippi, despite her family's best efforts to shield her from its worst aspects. Among other themes, the novel also examines the characters' **attachment to the land**, **family roots**, **independence** and the **self-respect** that comes from owning parcels of land.

Top Tip

Choose a passage that moves you from a text that you are reading and try to work out how the writer created the mood and atmosphere of the passage.

Mood and atmosphere

Writers try to create a mood and atmosphere in stories and novels to **illuminate the feelings and actions of their characters**. Mood and atmosphere, through the skilful use of description, helps to **set the tone** for a piece of writing. This creates a **frame of mind** for the reader and a **sense of expectation of what is to follow**.

Mood and atmosphere can be achieved by using the following literary effects:

the **careful choice of words** (diction) helps to suggest an atmosphere and tone

the **length and variety** of sentences; for example, short ones can suggest tension

repetition in sentences of words and phrases

similes (comparisons using 'as' or 'like')
metaphors (stronger comparisons in which you say something *is* something else)

monologues (speaking to oneself) and dreams and day-dreams are good ways of revealing the motives and desires of characters

personification (giving human feelings to animals or inanimate objects)

oxymorons (combining contradictory words and phrases to cause an effect)

assonance (combining words with rhyming vowel sounds, e.g. fowl owl)

alliteration (using words together that repeat the first sound of the word, e.g. lovely lush leaves)

motifs (words, ideas and imagery which recur in texts)

the use of the **senses**: sound, touch, sight, smell and taste

the **tone** of the narrator and his or her closeness to, or distance from, the action

(Some of the above effects are explained in more detail on pages 54–55.)

Dialogue

In novels, dialogue is more than mere communication: it makes characters seem more vivid and lifelike.

Characters' **aims, motives, personalities** and **outlooks** are revealed through what they say and the words and phrases that they use. Dialogue shows **what characters think about other characters**. This also helps us to make up our minds about them, and to understand how they relate to the main themes, messages and ideas in a story.

Third-person narration

The following is an example of third-person narration and characterisation from Doris Lessing's *Flight*:

He moved warily along the hedge, stalking his granddaughter, who was now looped over the gate, her head loose on her arms, singing. The light happy sound mingled with the crooning of the birds, and his anger mounted.

'Hey!' he shouted; saw her jump, look back, and abandon the gate.

Her eyes veiled themselves, and she said in a pert neutral voice: 'Hullo, Grandad.' Politely she moved towards him, after a lingering backward glance at the road.

'Waiting for Steven, hey?' he said, his fingers curling like claws into his palm.

'Any objection?' she asked lightly, refusing to look at him.

He confronted her, his eyes narrowed, shoulders hunched, tight in a hard knot of pain which included the preening birds, the sunlight, the flowers. He said: 'Think you're old enough to go courting, hey?'

First-person narration

The following is an example of first-person narration and dialogue from Sylvia Plath's *Superman and Paula Brown's New Snowsuit*. (The narrator has been wrongfully accused of spoiling Paula Brown's snowsuit.)

A mouthful of chocolate pudding blocked my throat, thick and bitter. I had to wash it down with milk. Finally I said, 'I didn't do it.'

But the words came out like hard, dry little seeds, hollow and insincere. I tried again. 'I didn't do it. Jimmy Lane did it.'

'Of course we'll believe you,' Mother said slowly, 'but the whole neighbourhood is talking about it. Mrs Sterling heard the story from Mrs Fein and sent David over to say we should buy Paula a new snowsuit. I can't understand it.'

'I didn't do it,' I repeated, and the blood beat in my ears like a slack drum. I pushed my chair away from the table, not looking at Uncle Frank or Mother sitting there, solemn and sorrowful in the candlelight.

The staircase to the second floor was dark, but I went down the long hall to my room without turning on the light switch and shut the door. A small unripe moon was shafting squares of greenish light along the floor and the window-panes were fringed with frost.

Quick Test

1. Theme refers to:
   a) the storyline of a novel or short story
   b) the overall topic that the writer is exploring
   c) the end of a story

2. Short sentences might create what kind of mood in prose writing?

3. Why is dialogue important for establishing characters?

4. What is first-person narration?

5. As well as identifying literary terms and techniques, what else must you do?

Answers 1. (b) **2.** Tension. **3.** To make them more interesting and real. **4.** Where the story is being told directly by one of the characters, e.g. 'I entered the room.' **5.** Comment on how effectively they have been used.

Short stories

Using short stories in the folio

When writing a critical evaluation of a short story for a folio piece, it is important that you **do more than simply re-tell the narrative** of the text (storyline).

Attention must be paid to features such as **dialogue**, **characterisation**, **setting**, and **theme**. The endings of many short stories contain 'twists' that also would invite comment in a critical essay.

Pay particular attention to the *Details of task*, as set out by your teacher and attempt to **deal with the specific requirements of the assignment**.

A folio task might look like this:

Details of task

Write about a short story that you thought was unusual in some way but which had an important message. Consider the writer's use of language, setting, structure, character, incident, humour and imagery. Remember to state your overall opinion of the story.

How to plan your essay

Look at the essay plan below, which uses the short story 'Hunter of Dryburn'
by Brian McCabe, to respond to this task.

Creating an essay plan becomes straightforward if you use the task as a guide.

Once your paragraph plan is created, use PEC to write the full essay.

Hunter of Dryburn

In this short story, which is written in Scots, a lonely man holds a one-sided conversation with a young couple who have inadvertently ended up in the village of Dryburn and have gone into a local pub for a drink. It becomes clear that the man, the 'hunter' of the title, is searching for some greater purpose to his life but appears to be trapped by the circumstances of living in a 'dump' like Dryburn.

Hunter of
Dryburn

Brian McCabe

The essay plan

Paragraph 1: Introduction

Use the task to help you write your opening paragraph. Give the **title** and **author** and say what you intend to do in your essay, e.g.

> *'Hunter of Dryburn' by Brain McCabe is a short story that I thought was unusual in a number of ways but which contained an important message. In this essay I will look at the writer's use of language, setting, structure, character, incident, humour and imagery and consider how effective he has been in conveying his viewpoint.*

Paragraph 2: 'language'

Explain what you thought was **unusual** about the story, e.g. that it was written in Scots. Say how this added to your enjoyment and how it made the characters realistic. Remember to **use some quotations**.

Paragraph 3: 'setting'

Write about the setting. **Explain how** we know that 'Dryburn's a dump' and **why** Dryburn is a good name for the village.

Paragraph 4: 'structure'

Now **explain** the unusual structure of the story, i.e. that it is a **dramatic monologue. Quote examples** of how the writer lets you know that other people are there.

Paragraph 5: 'character'

Write about the character of the Auld Man. Explain how we know why he was like this.

Paragraph 6: 'incident'

There is one **central incident** in the story – the auld man's death. Say what happened and **give your opinion** about who was to blame.

Paragraph 7: 'humour'

Give examples of the funny parts in the story and say how they added to you enjoyment.

Paragraph 8: 'imagery'

Now deal with the end of the story and the fact that the storyteller can't imagine a lion. **Explain** the point that the writer is trying to make. Give your overall opinion of the story.

Top Tip
It is much easier to write a good essay when you have enjoyed a story. If you are given a choice, pick a favourite text.

Top Tip
Remember to give examples and use quotations from the text to back up your point.

Quick Test

1. What are the most popular areas for comparison between two short stories?
2. Why should you pick a text you have enjoyed when writing a critical essay?

Answers 1. Character and theme. **2.** It will be easier to write about.

Test your progress

Use the questions to test your progress.
Check your answers at the back of the book on page 95.

1. What does 'plot' mean?

   ....

2. What does it mean to 'contrast'?

   ....

3. Explain the term 'genre'.

   ....

4. What is meant by a 'writer's craft'?

   ....

5. Explain what 'irony' means.

   ....

6. What are 'transitions'?

   ....

7. What are the main styles of narration?

   ....

8. From which viewpoint does a first-person narrator tell a story?

   ....

9. Does the author believe what a narrator believes?

   ....

10. What type of narrator can see most in a story?

   ....

11. Give three ways of understanding a character.

   ....

12. What is an 'omniscient narrator'?

   ....

13. What is meant by the terms 'flat' and 'round' characters?

   ....

14. Define what 'dialogue' means.

   ....

15. Why do writers use dialogue?

   ....

16. Briefly explain the rules for how dialogue should be set out on the page.

....

17. What is a monologue?

....

18. How can dialogue help you to learn more about characters?

....

19. Identify three similarities in novels and short stories.

....

20. Point out three differences between short stories and novels.

....

21. Why do short stories concentrate on mainly one plot?

....

22. Point out three ways in which writers create mood and atmosphere in their stories.

....

23. What is 'diction'?

....

24. Mood and atmosphere sets up a frame of mind and an expectation of what is to follow in a text. True or false?

....

25. Mood and atmosphere can be achieved through the skilful use of description or imagery. True or false?

....

26. Imagery is used only for poetry and not in novels or short stories. True or false?

....

27. Explain the difference between 'alliteration' and 'assonance'.

....

28. What is a theme?

....

How did you do?		
1–9 correct	....	start again
10–15 correct	....	getting there
16–22 correct	....	good work
23–28 correct	....	excellent

Critical evaluations

What you may study

The play that you study will be determined by what your English teachers have in their library; Shakespeare's *Macbeth*, the 'Scottish play', is a popular choice.

As you read the play, try to get the gist of what characters are saying before you read passages again for a more detailed understanding. Also make use of any general notes in your books to guide your understanding.

How you will be graded

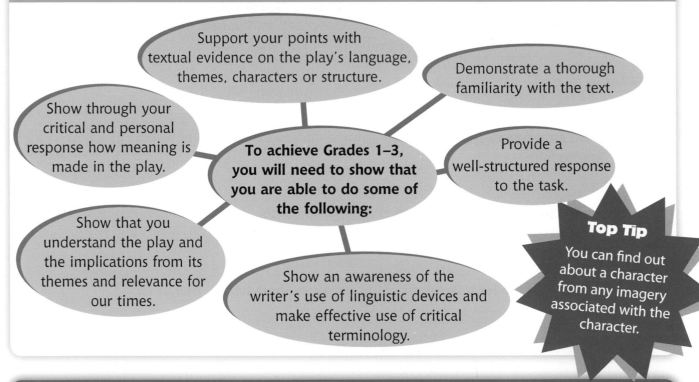

Support your points with textual evidence on the play's language, themes, characters or structure.

Demonstrate a thorough familiarity with the text.

Show through your critical and personal response how meaning is made in the play.

To achieve Grades 1–3, you will need to show that you are able to do some of the following:

Provide a well-structured response to the task.

Show that you understand the play and the implications from its themes and relevance for our times.

Show an awareness of the writer's use of linguistic devices and make effective use of critical terminology.

Top Tip

You can find out about a character from any imagery associated with the character.

Writing a critical evaluation on a play by Shakespeare

The plays most often studied are:

- *Julius Caesar*
- *The Merchant of Venice*
- *Macbeth*
- *The Tempest*
- *Romeo and Juliet*
- *A Midsummer Night's Dream*
- *Twelfth Night*

Shakespeare's choice of language

Shakespeare used **three styles of writing** in his plays. Here are a few examples from *Twelfth Night*:

1: Poetic verse (rhymed)

Verse which is often used to signal the end of a scene, such as a curtain call, or for heightened dramatic effect. Take, for example, this rhyming couplet from *Twelfth Night*:

> *Duke Orsino:* Away before me to sweet beds of flowers:
> Love-thoughts lie rich when canopied with bowers.

2: Blank verse (unrhymed)

Verse intended to represent the rhythms of speech. It is usually used by noble characters, who are given elevated speech to show their feelings and mood:

> *Duke Orsino:* If music be the food of love, play on.

Note how the speech is in **iambic pentameter**. That is, it has ten syllables to the line in which five are stressed. The rhythm pattern is ti-tum, ti-tum, ti-tum, ti-tum, ti-tum. Sometimes you'll find more or fewer stresses to the lines, yet the overall pattern will be even.

3: Prose

Ordinary language used by characters of all ranks, but uneducated characters tend to use it. It can also be used for comic exchanges between characters, for plot development, and for speech which lacks dramatic intensity:

> *Viola as Cesario:* Save thee, friend, and thy music. Dost thou live by thy tabor?
>
> *Feste:* No, sir, I live by the church.
>
> *Viola:* Art thou a churchman?
>
> *Feste:* No such matter sir: I do live by the church; for I do live at my house, and my house doth stand by the church.

Quick Test

1. What are the three styles of writing used by Shakespeare?

2. How do you support points made in a critical essay?

3. What is poetic verse often used to signal?

4. What is blank verse intended to represent?

Answers 1. Poetic verse, blank verse and prose. **2.** By producing textual evidence. **3.** The end of an act or a scene. **4.** The natural rhythms of speech.

Shakespeare – structure and theme

Plot structure

Shakespeare liked to stress the comedy or seriousness of many scenes within his plays by making **dramatic contrasts**. He did this by **placing a serious scene after a comic scene** and vice versa.

Main characters are introduced to the audience. **Order reigns** and the world and nature are in natural harmony.

Problems are revealed. Things begin to go wrong. Confusions, murders, deceit, pranks and other complications begin.

As events progress there is **chaos** and **a loss of order and harmony**. The natural world appears out of sorts.

Things come to a head in the play's **climax**. ('Climax' comes from the Greek word for 'ladder'.) If you are reading a tragedy, then several more deaths occur now, including a main character like Macbeth. The climax is the moment of the **highest dramatic intensity in the play**, particularly for the main character.

Order is re-established with the right people in control again. Nature is again at one with the main characters. Comedies usually end in several, usually three, marriages.

Conflict

As with any play **conflict** is a **central concern** in Shakespeare's texts. This can take a number of forms:

Perhaps the most obvious source of conflict is when **the central figure is in a direct clash with another major character**. Whatever the source of conflict, the play will work towards **the resolution of the conflict** in its narrative / storyline.

Conflict can be within a single character who is **torn between two desires**.

A writer may use a number of characters to explore a **basic clash between two ideas**, e.g. good and evil.

Themes

Shakespeare's plays are rich with thematic content and **often several issues will be explored** within a single text. A number of themes also appear in more than one play.

Recurring thematic concerns of Shakespeare include:

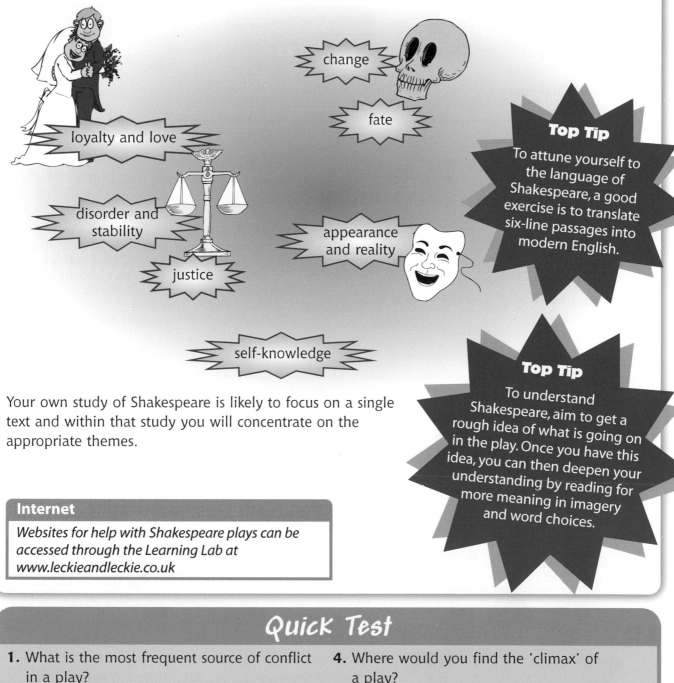

- loyalty and love
- change
- fate
- disorder and stability
- justice
- appearance and reality
- self-knowledge

Top Tip

To attune yourself to the language of Shakespeare, a good exercise is to translate six-line passages into modern English.

Top Tip

To understand Shakespeare, aim to get a rough idea of what is going on in the play. Once you have this idea, you can then deepen your understanding by reading for more meaning in imagery and word choices.

Your own study of Shakespeare is likely to focus on a single text and within that study you will concentrate on the appropriate themes.

Internet

Websites for help with Shakespeare plays can be accessed through the Learning Lab at www.leckieandleckie.co.uk

Quick Test

1. What is the most frequent source of conflict in a play?

2. What function has the end of a play in terms of conflict?

3. What is a theme?

4. Where would you find the 'climax' of a play?

5. What does 'plot' mean?

6. What does 'context' mean?

7. What is 'textual evidence'?

Answers 1. Between two characters. **2.** To resolve the main conflict. **3.** It is the play's main message or idea. There can be several themes in a play. **4.** Near the end. **5.** The plan or outline of the play. **6.** The events and ideas around at the time when the text was written. **7.** Brief quotations from the play that are used as evidence for points in essays.

Shakespeare – imagery

Figures of speech

Shakespeare uses figures of speech – that is, imagery or word pictures – to do the following:

| say more about points made in dialogue and action | reinforce and enhance the audience's ideas of the characters | magnify or draw attention to themes or issues in the text |

To do this, Shakespeare uses:

Motifs

Motifs are characters, themes or images that **recur** throughout a text. For example, disguise is a running idea in *Twelfth Night*. In *Macbeth* there are several motifs. One is 'fair and foul' and another is sleep:

- To the Weird Sisters, who characterise evil, what is ugly is beautiful, and what is beautiful is ugly: 'Fair is foul and foul is fair.'

- Macbeth and Lady Macbeth reign in restless ecstasy after murdering King Duncan. Macbeth soon says to illustrate the sleep motif:

Me thought I heard a voice cry, "Sleep no more!"
Macbeth does murder sleep – the innocent sleep,
Sleep that knits up the ravelled sleave of care,
The death of each day's life, sore labour's bath,
Balm of hurt minds, great nature's second course
Chief nourisher in life's feast.
(Macbeth, Act 2, Scene 2, lines 34–39)

Similes

Similes are comparisons using 'as' or 'like'; for example: 'The moon is like a balloon.'

Metaphors

Stronger comparisons saying something *is* something else: 'The moon is a balloon', 'The world is a stage.'

Personification

Giving human feelings to animals or inanimate objects: 'The sun smiled.'

Oxymorons

These are words and phrases that you would not expect to see yoked together to cause an effect. For example, as soon as Juliet hears that Tybalt, her cousin, has been killed by Romeo, her grief and outrage is tempered by her disbelief that Romeo could carry out such a deed: 'Fiend angelical, dove-feathered raven, wolvish-ravening lamb, ... A damned saint, an honourable villain!' *(Romeo and Juliet, Act 3, Scene 2, lines 75–79)*

Top Tip
Get a recording of a play from your local library and listen to parts of the play as it is read. It will help your understanding.

Extended Metaphors

A metaphor that is used extensively throughout a passage.

An example of Shakespeare's imagery

In the following speech from *King Lear*, Kent is enquiring of a Gentleman whether Cordelia, the daughter of King Lear, has been upset by a letter describing her father's condition.

Kent:	O, then it mov'd her?
Gentleman:	Not to a rage. Patience and sorrow strove
	Who should express her goodliest. You have seen
	Sunshine and rain at once: her smiles and tears
	Were like a better way. Those happy smilets
	That play'd on her ripe lip seem'd not to know
	What guests were in her eyes, which parted thence
	As pearls from diamonds dropp'd. In brief,
	Sorrow would be a rarity most belov'd,
	If all could so become it.

King Lear, Act 4, Scene 3

Top Tip

If the audience knows more about the development of the plot than the characters do, then this is known as **dramatic irony**.

The Gentleman attempts to describe Cordelia's **conflicting** emotions in a number of ways. First he uses **personification** to make the struggle in her mind between patience and sorrow seem more vivid.

He then moves on to **metaphors** of 'sunshine' and 'rain' to express these emotions. In order to give an impression of the strength of her emotions, he again uses **personification** to characterise the smilets (small smiles) that 'played' on her lips, and the tears that were 'guests' in her eyes. Finally, he uses a simile to describe the richness and beauty of Cordelia's tears, which part from her eyes as 'pearls from diamonds dropp'd'.

This moment is very moving. It is an example of Shakespeare's dramatic technique that he has Cordelia's reaction described rather than calling upon an actor to play it.

Quick Test

Circle the correct answer:

1. Shakespeare uses imagery:
   a) to make his writing pretty
   b) to fill up space
   c) to enhance our understanding of a character, theme or point

2. A simile is a figure of speech which:
   a) draws a comparison using 'as' or 'like'
   b) allows characters to smile
   c) has to do with singularity
   d) makes a comparison using 'is' or 'are'

3. The term 'imagery' means:
   a) looking in mirrors
   b) word pictures
   c) writing prose

Answers 1. (c) 2. (a) 3. (b)

Using PEC

PEC for critical evaluation

In all your critical evaluations, it is important that you consider the words of the task carefully. This will give your essay a clear sense of purpose, which is one of the key features that a marker will be looking for.

Consider the example below, which is based on the play *An Inspector Calls* by J.B. Priestley and illustrates how you should approach critical evaluation.

Details of task

Choose a play that you feel has an important social message for our time. Consider in some detail how the dramatist uses the issue of conflict between the characters to explore the theme. How successful has the dramatist been?

Firstly, use a spidergram (mind-map) to plan your work.

Top Tip

As with any genre, when you write essays on plays you should use the PEC method:
- make a point
- give evidence for your point
- comment on your evidence.

What the message is – social responsibility

Title: 'How J.B. Priestley uses conflict between his characters to explore an important social message.'

Conflict between:
Goole and Mr Birling
Goole and Gerard
Goole and Sheila
Goole and Eric
Goole and Mrs Birling

Other conflicts:
Sheila and Eric and their parents
Sheila and Gerard

Introduction

Use the words of the task to assist with your opening paragraph. In the following example, the underlined words have been lifted from the task.

> A <u>play that has an important social message for our time</u> is 'An Inspector Calls' by J.B. Priestley. In this essay <u>I will consider in some detail how the dramatist uses the issue of conflict between the characters to explore the theme</u> of social responsibility and comment on <u>how successful he has been.</u>

Now, using PEC, you can begin to write the body of your essay:

Point

> A key conflict in the drama is between Inspector Goole and Mr Birling. The writer uses this clash to illustrate the uncaring nature of Mr Birling and men like him.

Explanation

> The Inspector accuses Birling of having unfairly sacked a young female worker for simply standing up for her rights. Birling is unrepentant, however, and justifies his sacking of the girl by saying: 'She'd had a lot to say – far too much – she had to go.' When told that this act was the first in a chain of events that apparently led to the girl's tragic suicide, Birling remains defiant: 'I can't accept any responsibility.'

Comment

> However, it is clear that the Inspector feels that Birling, and the others at the dinner party he interrupted, need to learn to take responsibility for those around them. He says, later, 'We are members of one body. We are responsible for each other.' This is the important social message that the writer wishes us to learn.

Repeat this pattern for the other key points from your plan.

Conclusion

It is important in your conclusion to draw together the key points of the task and to highlight your personal evaluation of the writer's success:

> J.B. Priestley has been extremely successful in using conflict between his characters to explore the central theme of social responsibility. Although the play was written over fifty years ago and is set during an even earlier period, the message that we need to consider ourselves as members of one community, one world, has never been more relevant.

Top Tip

Keep quotations relevant and brief. Aim to use single words and phrases, and certainly no more than a sentence or two, to prove your points. Remember to comment on the quotations that you use.

Quick Test

1. What does PEC stand for?
2. What should you back up your points with?
3. What is the purpose of the conclusion?

Test your progress

Use the questions to test your progress.
Check your answers at the back of the book on page 95.

1. Name two possible sources of conflict in a play.

   ....

2. What must you remember to do with any quotations you use?

   ....

3. What are the main genres of Shakespeare plays?

   ....

4. List the three styles of writing Shakespeare used in his plays.

   ....

5. Where did Shakespeare use poetic verse?

   ....

6. What is the purpose of blank verse?

   ....

7. What does Shakespeare like to establish at the beginning of his plays?

   ....

8. What happens next?

   ....

9. What is the 'climax' of a play?

   ....

10. What could happen during the climax of a play?

    ....

11. Briefly explain what usually happens at the end of a Shakespeare play.

    ....

12. What is a 'theme'?

    ....

13. Identify three themes that can be found in Shakespeare's plays.

    ....

14. What type of themes might you expect to find in a comedy?

    ....

15. Briefly explain what is meant by 'dramatic contrast'.

    ....

16. Why did Shakespeare build dramatic contrasts into his plays?

....

17. Explain what is meant by 'self-knowledge'.

....

18. Briefly sum up the typical structure of a Shakespeare play.

....

19. What is meant by the term 'figure of speech'?

....

20. What is a simile?

....

21. Why is a metaphor a stronger comparison?

....

22. What is an extended metaphor?

....

23. What is meant by 'personification'?

....

24. Define an oxymoron.

....

25. What is a motif?

....

26. Give two reasons why Shakespeare uses imagery in his plays.

....

27. Shakespeare uses a great deal of irony in his plays. What is irony?

....

28. What is dramatic irony?

....

29. Why and where would you expect to find passages rich in imagery?

....

30. Briefly sum up what is meant by imagery.

....

How did you do?

1–9	correct	start again
10–15	correct	getting there
16–25	correct	good work
26–30	correct	excellent

Studying poetry

Chaucer SHELLEY WORDSWORTH t.s eliot coleridge Keats

What you have to study

Poetry is a significant part of Standard Grade English courses. Typically, at least one of your Reading folio pieces will be in response to a poem (the maximum number will be two).

The **type of poems** that you will study will range extensively, from **ballads** (narrative or story poems) to **sonnets** (serious poems that explore deep themes, such as love and death) to **free verse**.

You will be expected to make considered responses to them on the basis of content, theme and technique.

Responding to a poem

Study the poem very carefully.

- Consider briefly **what you think the poem is about**. You are looking for an **overview** at this stage. This early view of the poem may change once you have studied it in greater detail.

- Examine **how the poet gets their meaning across** through their choice of **form, language, imagery** and **themes**.

- Consider the poem's **tone**. For example, what is the **attitude** of the speaker towards the topic or theme? What is their attitude to you? Does the poem's tone change in the poem? Go through each area as fully as you can.

- Once you have studied the text, **consider your views again** on the poem, stating what the poem is about. Consider, in particular, **what you may have learned** from the poem.

Top Tip

Do not merely identify figures of speech and other poetic techniques, but show how they affect meaning in the poem.

Top Tip

Try to write a poem of your own using a specific form – there is a lot to be learned about poetry by trying to write your own poem. You may even find that you enjoy writing poetry.

How you will be graded

Show that you have **engaged with the poems** by giving a sustained and developed response to key words and phrases in your task. More sophisticated answers will display an **enthusiastic personal response** with **close textual analysis**.

Display **analytical and interpretive skills** when examining the **social, moral and philosophical significance** of the poem.

Explore the poems and **show insight**. Again, more sophisticated responses will show greater insight or exploration of the poems.

To achieve Grades 1–3, you will need to:

Give a **sophisticated personal response** that is **convincing and imaginative**, showing a high degree of **empathy**.

Explain how the poet has **used language and imagery** in the poem. In other words, you will need to be able to **identify word choices** (**diction**) and what they may suggest. You should also show how the poet uses **figures of speech**, such as similes, to add meaning to his or her **ideas and messages** in the poem(s).

Identify with the **poet's intentions** or the **view of the narrator** in the poem.

Say something about **the poet's purposes and intentions**. What is the poet setting out to achieve?

Quick Test

1. How many folio pieces may be in response to poetry?
2. What kind of poem is a ballad?
3. What is empathy?

Answers 1. 2 **2.** A narrative poem. **3.** Identifying with the theme or idea in a poem or perhaps the narrator's point of view.

Writing about poetry

Tips on writing about poetry

One of the biggest problems in writing about poetry is finding phrases that enable you to express your ideas and make your writing flow. You should aim to **integrate useful phrases** into your writing so that you can explain yourself with ease in critical essays. Beware, however, of always using the same phrases, which would lead to a mechanical style.

The following framework is not really meant as a substitute for your structure, but to provide a helping hand if you get stuck.

- **Introduce points** that you want to make by using some of the phrases given below; change them around or simply add them together. The more fluent you are the more impressive your points will be.

- Good grades in critical evaluations are achieved through **knowing your texts** and being able to **express your points in a fluent manner**. You will also be judged on your **punctuation**, **use of language** and the **quality of your expression**.

- Look out for **useful ways of expressing your ideas** and make a note of them. Successful pupils are able to make their points in essays in a fluent and knowledgeable manner.

1: Introductory phrases

- The poem … is about …

- The poem is narrated in the first / second person. This enhances the poem's meaning because …

- The form of the poem is (a ballad / sonnet / two-, three-, four-, five-line stanzas / free verse) … This is an appropriate form for the poem because it helps readers to appreciate …

Top Tip

Remember PEC:
- make a **point** to address your question
- give a word, phrase or line of **evidence** for it
- **comment** on your evidence and link it to the task.

Top Tip

It is important to be precise when writing about poetry. Remember that 'verse' means the whole poem or a collection of poems. You should use 'stanza' when you want to describe a part of a poem, such as a four-line 'quatrain'.

2: Phrases for the middle of a piece of writing

- The theme / idea of ... is present / repeated in both poems. For example, the poet contrasts ... with ...

- The poet uses appropriate language to convey a feeling of ... For example ...

- The caesura after ... helps an audience to understand that ...

- The use of alliteration / assonance / onomatopoeia with ... shows that ...

- The poet's use of imagery (similes / metaphors / personification) can be seen with ... This shows / intensifies the idea of ...

- Another interesting example of this is ... This emphasises / shows / reinforces / gives a sense of / refers to ...

- The poem's meaning is enhanced / deepened with ... An example of which is ...

- This refers to the main idea of ... For example, this can be seen with ... .

- The poem reflects the narrator's / poet's feelings on ... of ...

- The poet reminds the reader of ... with ...

- The poet draws attention to the fact that ...

- The poet compares ... with ...

3: Phrases to sum up your arguments and views

- The poem's / narrator's tone is one of ... This helps the reader / audience to appreciate the/ how ...

- From reading these poems I learned that ...

- The tone(s) in each poem is / are ... This / these show(s) that ...

- To sum up, I would say that the poet feels ... about his / her subject. The poet wants us to understand / feel the ...

- My final view of the poem(s) is that it is / they are ...

- Both / each of the poems show ... This shows the poet's feelings of ...

Quick Test

1. What does PEC stand for?
2. Find out what the term 'caesura' means.
3. Find out the number of lines in a sonnet.
4. What is alliteration?
5. What is a writing frame?

Answers 1. Point – Evidence – Comment. **2.** A 'cut'; the term refers to any punctuation mark used in poetry. **3.** 14 **4.** Repetition of consonants for an effect; for example, the headline, 'Football Fever.' **5.** A structured bank of phrases designed to help your writing flow.

Poetic techniques

Discussing poetic technique

For a poetic form (sonnet, dramatic monologue) essay, you need to:

- have a good grasp of the rules of the form, e.g. rhyme scheme or use of persona
- be able to discuss how each poem uses the form
- be able to discuss how the poets adapt the form for their own purposes
- be able to assess the effectiveness of the use of the form.

Top Tip

Make sure you show **how** poetic techniques add meaning to a poem.

Some essential poetic terms

Use of letter and word sounds

Alliteration: the same consonant at the beginning of words repeated for an effect, e.g. *fireside flickers*.

Assonance: repetition of vowel sounds for an effect, e.g. *icy winds knife us*. The repetition of the vowel 'i' helps stress the coldness of the 'winds'.

Onomatopoeia: words which sound like their meaning, e.g. *buzz* and *click*.

Rhythm and rhyme: the poem's pace when read aloud, and word endings that sound alike for an effect.

Imagery

Metaphor: a strong comparison where 'is' or 'are' is used or implied. *Juliet is the sun.*

Personification ('person-making'): giving an animal, idea or object human feelings to enhance an emotion, feeling or effect, e.g. *Arise fair sun and kill the envious moon*.

Oxymoron: figures of speech in which contradictory, opposite words are yoked together for an effect. For example, The Beatles, the great 1960s' pop band, famously had a hit song and a film entitled *A Hard Day's Night*. Oxymorons can also be **paradoxes** to enliven prose, but some have turned into clichés, e.g. *act naturally, living dead*, etc.

Simile: a comparison using 'as' or 'like', e.g. *My love is as deep as the sea*.

Punctuation and form

Ballad: a story poem that usually features dramatic stories about ordinary people.

Couplet: a two-line stanza that rhymes.

Verse: an entire poem or collection of poems or poetry.

Caesura (or cesura): means 'a cutting'. It can be any type of punctuation in poetry that causes the reader to pause. Poets use them to end-stop their lines and to emphasise points and ideas in their poetry. A caesura can add a great deal of meaning if placed in the middle of a line.

Elegy: a poem for a dead person.

Enjambment (or run-on line or stanza): one line runs into another to achieve a poetic effect. It is often used to aid rhythm and help enact something.

Free verse: irregular stanzas filled with lines of varying length. The lines are like waves coming in along a sea-shore: each has natural rhythm and is just long enough. The form suits conversational and argumentative poems. Free verse, or *vers libre*, was the most popular form of poetry in the twentieth century and remains so today.

Lyric: a poem that sets out the thoughts and feelings of a single speaker.

Quatrain: four lines of a poem that rhyme. It is the main unit in English poetry.

Stanza: a clear section of a poem, usually two or four lines.

Sonnet: usually a 14-line poem about a serious theme such as love or death.

Triplet (or tercet): a three-line stanza. It is a form suited for comic poetry. Poets sometimes reverse the expected content, e.g. Seamus Heaney's 'Mid-Term Break'. The effect can be very poignant.

Narrative stance and attitudes within poems

Dramatic monologue is a poem spoken by the first-person narrator, who is not the poet. The poet adopts a persona and addresses an unspeaking implied listener. A dramatic monologue is often written in the present tense, as in a speech made on stage.

Robert Browning's 'My Last Duchess' is a well-known poem in Scottish schools that uses dramatic monologue. The poem is spoken by a Renaissance duke who had his last wife killed for being too easily pleased and not appreciating his aristocratic heritage. The implied listener is an ambassador who has come to arrange the duke's next marriage. The poem makes good use of a dramatic situation – the two men are looking at a portrait of the duchess and the persona's attitude is cruel. There is an interesting use of run-on lines and rhyme.

Tone: a poet's or a narrator's attitude towards their subject and audience. Tone can change within a poem to emphasise changes of meaning.

The poet's use of diction (words deliberately chosen for their associations and sounds) can affect the **tone** of a poem. Contrasts between multi-syllable and one-syllable words can very quickly change the mood of a poem. In Carol Ann Duffy's poem 'Education for Leisure', the contrast between the multi-syllabic 'pavements suddenly glitter' and the mono-syllabic 'I touch your arm' is very chilling.

Internet

Links to useful exercises, ideas and help with poetry and texts can be found at Leckie and Leckie's Learning Lab.

Quick Test

1. What is a simile?
2. Explain what empathy means.
3. Give an example of onomatopoeia.
4. What is the difference between 'verse' and a 'stanza'?
5. What is a suitable subject for a sonnet and why?

Answers 1. A comparison using 'as' or 'like'. **2.** An appreciation of a writer's or narrator's concerns and ideas. **3.** Any word that sounds like its meaning, e.g. buzz. **4.** 'Verse' is an entire poem or collection of poems; a 'stanza' is a section of a poem. **5.** 'Love' or 'death' because sonnets usually have serious subject matter.

Two poems to study

Six O'Clock News

this is thi
six a clock
news thi
man said n
thi reason
a talk wia
BBC accent
iz coz yi
widny wahnt
mi ti talk
aboot thi
trooth wia
voice lik
wanna yoo
scruff. if
a toktaboot
thi trooth
lik wanna yoo
scruff yi
widny thingk
it wuz troo.
jist wanna yoo
scruff tokn.
thirza right
way ti spell
ana right way
ti tok it. this
is me tokn yir
right way a
spellin. this
is ma trooth.
yooz doant no
thi trooth
yirsellz cawz
yi canny talk
right. this is
the six a clock
nyooz. belt up.

Tom Leonard

Half-Caste

Excuse me
standing on one leg
I'm half-caste

Explain yuself
what yu mean
when yu say half-caste
yu mean when picasso
mix red an green
is a half-caste canvas
explain yuself
wha yu mean
when yu say half-caste
yu mean when light an shadow
mix in de sky
is a half-caste weather
well in dat case
england weather
nearly always half-caste
in fact some o dem cloud
half-caste till dem overcast
so spiteful dem dont want de sun pass
ah rass
explain yuself
wha yu mean
when yu say half-caste
yu mean tchaikovsky
sit down at dah piano
an mix a black key
wid a white key
is a half-caste symphony

Explain yuself
wha yu mean
Ah listening to yu wid de keen
half of mih ear
Ah lookin at yu wid de keen
half of mih eye
and when I'm introduced to yu

I'm sure you'll understand
why I offer yu half-a-hand
an when I sleep at night
I close half-a-eye
consequently when I dream
I dream half-a-dream
an when moon begin to glow
I half-caste human being
cast half-a-shadow
but yu must come back tomorrow
wid de whole of yu eye
an de whole of yu ear
an de whole of yu mind

an I will tell yu
de other half
of my story

John Agard

What the poems are about

1. Both poems deal with issues of **language**, **power** and **prejudice**.

2. Leonard ironically **reverses the usual dialects** associated with authority and reading the news (received pronunciation and standard English). He wants us to think about issues of truth and authority when we only hear the news read by people with received pronunciation or standard English.

3. Leonard argues that it is wrong and prejudiced to believe that these dialects are the only ones capable of expressing the truth and so be taken seriously.

4. The **tone** of Leonard's poem is one of **anger against the prejudices** of society where working-class dialects are not taken seriously and given no respect.

5. Agard's narrator eloquently shows, through a number of unusual and convincing comparisons, that it is **wrong to label anyone by using the term 'half-caste'**. The unquestioned use of such terms can lead to **prejudice**.

6. Agard and Leonard show us that **power**, **authority** and **prejudice are linked with language and how we use it**. They warn us against blindly accepting some dialects, such as standard English, as voices of authority and correctness while excluding others and their speakers as only worthy of ridicule. **The 'truth' can be expressed in other dialects too.**

How meaning is expressed

1. The impact of each poem's argument is enhanced through being spoken by a **first-person narrator**.

2. Both poems are appropriately set out in **free verse**, in which the **dialect is defiantly proclaimed and phonetically spelled** in lines of varying length. The narrowness of the poems' lines contrast with other poems written in standard English.

3. The rules of standard English have no place in these poems as there is **no punctuation, nor capital letters**. The narrators make their points with **questions**, **arguments** and **statements** and to advance an alternative to standard English. Agard's poem has stanzas in which some of **the senses are alluded to**. Leonard's poem is plainer, using a single stanza or verse paragraph to refer to speech and Glaswegian dialect. The poets are from different parts of the world yet have similar views on language, about what should be said and how it should be expressed.

4. Both poems have an ironic tone intended to startle their audiences into accepting the truth of the arguments that they advance.

Quick Test

1. What is the term for words that make the sound they are describing?

2. 'Winter spread its icy grip across the land' – What type of figurative language is demonstrated here?

3. What do we call a poem that is written for a person who is dead?

4. What is the main unit of English poetry?

5. How many lines does a sonnet contain?

Answers 1. Onomatopoeia. **2.** Personification. **3.** Elegy. **4.** Quatrain. **5.** 14

Test your progress

Use the questions to test your progress.
Check your answers at the back of the book on page 95.

1. How many critical essays on poetry may you include in your folio?

....

2. Are you being tested on your reading or your writing?

....

3. Name two forms for poems.

....

4. What is tone?

....

5. What are the main forms of narration?

....

6. Diction is another word for the word choices that poets make for their poems. True or false?

....

7. What is a theme?

....

8. Part of a poem is a verse. True or false?

....

9. The classroom 'glowed like a sweet shop' is a metaphor. True or false?

....

10. What is 'enjambment'?

....

11. What does it mean to 'compare and contrast' when writing about poetry?

....

12. What is an oxymoron?

....

13. What can an oxymoron suggest?

....

14. Quatrains are the main units of English poetry. True or false?

....

15. What is free verse?

....

16. Why is free verse appropriate for certain poems?

....

17. What is assonance?

....

18. Where should you give your personal view of the poems that you write about?

....

19. Once you identify a figure of speech or some other poetic technique, what must you do afterwards?

....

20. What is imagery in a poem?

....

How did you do?

1–9	correct	start again
10–15	correct	getting there
16–20	correct	excellent

A critical essay task for you to tackle

Write a critical essay comparing 'Half-Caste' by John Agard and 'Six O'Clock News' by Tom Leonard. Consider in particular the importance of language and form in the poems and how they help to convey the essential message of both texts.

Talking and listening

What you are expected to do

You will need to do a range of targeted assessments in class for the talking component of the course covering individual and group situations.

Individual talk

When you are doing a solo talk, be clear as to the purpose of the talk. Is it:

- to convey information?
- to present an opinion or explore a topic?
- to describe a personal experience?

If you are given a free choice for an individual talk, try to pick a subject that only you could talk about. Choose something that you know really well and would enjoy talking about. Research and preparation are important aspects of an individual talk.

Group talk

There are two main types of assignment used for group talks:

1. **A task related to a text you are reading**. It might be to discuss a particular character or theme from the text, and much of your basic knowledge will come from how well you have studied the text in class. Note that in a discussion you are exchanging opinions – there is not necessarily a 'correct' answer. The key point is that you attempt to support your views with evidence.

2. **You are given a topic**, usually with some degree of topicality and even controversy. For example, you may have studied *Of Mice and Men* and your teacher sets you the task of discussing euthanasia, arising out of the book's ending. Do some **research** and **form opinions** on the topic before your assessment, as this will make it easier for you to contribute.

Top Tip

In group situations it is important that you take turns in speaking and show that you can listen! Do not talk over people.

How you will be graded

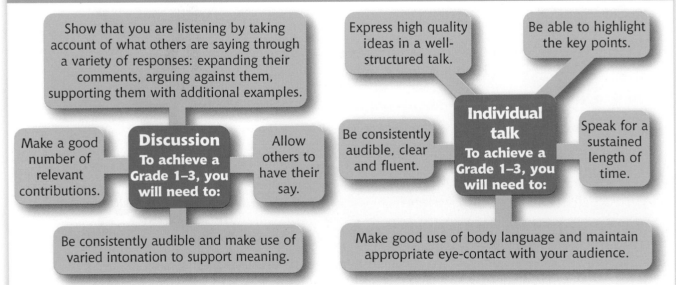

Show that you are listening by taking account of what others are saying through a variety of responses: expanding their comments, arguing against them, supporting them with additional examples.

Make a good number of relevant contributions.

Discussion
To achieve a Grade 1–3, you will need to:

Allow others to have their say.

Be consistently audible and make use of varied intonation to support meaning.

Express high quality ideas in a well-structured talk.

Be able to highlight the key points.

Be consistently audible, clear and fluent.

Individual talk
To achieve a Grade 1–3, you will need to:

Speak for a sustained length of time.

Make good use of body language and maintain appropriate eye-contact with your audience.

Hints for talking and listening

- Can you **speak with purpose in a structured way**? You need to **signpost your points** when you speak so that others can follow what you are saying and do not get bored.

- Are you able to **speak with fluency and confidence** on your chosen topic with minimal notes? **Do not make the mistake of reading your notes**.

- Do you **vary the sound of your voice to interest your audience**? Do you **use eye contact** and other **body language** to interest your listener? Sixty per cent of any communication is non-verbal! Use body language such as posture, hand gestures and eye contact, and vary the **tone and pitch of your voice**.

- Can you adapt the **register of your speech** to the task and your audience? You would hardly speak to your head teacher using the same tone of voice as you would to your best friends. You need to be conscious of how people adapt their speech to those they are talking to.

- Are you able to **use language with confidence** in a range of situations? How fluent and clear is your English?

- Can you **initiate speech**, **sustain a point of view** or **manage the contributions of others**? If you can, you would make a great host of a discussion panel.

- Can you **listen with sensitivity** and **respond accordingly**? Are you able to carry forward and further the arguments of others and follow a complex conversation?

Can you show flair or make thought-provoking contributions?

Can you use rhetorical techniques?

Can you skilfully involve listeners?

Can you show that you have a wide vocabulary?

Quick Test

1. Why should you 'signpost' your talk?

2. What two ingredients are essential before you attempt an individual talk?

3. Who is in charge of a group talk?

4. Why must you speak clearly in a talk situation?

Answers 1. So that the audience can follow your argument. **2.** Research and preparation. **3.** The appointed Chairperson. **4.** So that others can understand you.

Giving a talk

Preparing your talk

1: Topic

Think of a suitable title for your talk – this will help you to focus on your topic.

Research your topic – talk to experts, do some research on the Internet, look in encyclopedias, check out your library, write to agencies, companies or embassies.

Gather resources to help you with the details, points and arguments of your talk. Find and prepare any props that you need; they will be useful for focusing and keeping your audience's attention on what you are saying.

2: Structure

Think about the structure of your talk: introduction, body and conclusion. Summarise the talk in a few paragraphs. Keep them brief. Brainstorm your talk into a flow chart.

3: Prompts

Cut up several square pieces of card just smaller than a postcard.

Write down your main ideas in words or phrases as memory prompts. Resist the temptation to write too much. Keep them brief.

Write the words or phrases twice the size of your normal writing. If you forget your next point, just glance at your card. Turn over the cards as you speak.

Number the cards in the right order. The structure of your talk will then be clear for you as well as for your audience.

4: Practice

- Practise your talk to get the structure and any specialised or unusual vocabulary clear in your mind.
- Practise speaking clearly and consider any places in your talk where you might pause and welcome questions. Questions could act as ice-breakers and help you to relax. You will also be able to gauge the impact of the early parts of your talk.
- **Practise any unusual or specialised vocabulary** so that you appear confident and do not stumble over topic-specific terms.
- Remember to get props or handouts ready if you need them.

Top Tip

Make sure that you practise your talk before you have to deliver it. Use your parents, your cat or even the mirror, but ensure that you have heard yourself before you attempt to speak to others.

Giving the talk

- Try to appear relaxed and confident. (Check the list of hints for talking and listening on page 71.)

- Stand up and try to appear lively by modulating your voice. Remember to match your talk to your audience.

- Speak as fluently and confidently as you can.

- Be prepared to field questions and show your understanding of your topic by answering them. Prepare beforehand by thinking about the kind of questions that you could be asked.

- Show that you can listen carefully and respond in a sympathetic manner to questions asked.

Self-evaluation

Evaluate your performance afterwards. What did you do well? What could you have done better? You should write down all the relevant details:

1. The date of your talk and its title.
2. Specify what type of talk it was.
3. Self-assess how your talk went. What did you do well? How did the audience respond to your talk?
4. Keep a written record of the teacher's feedback on your talk to help you improve your next one. Complete your record by identifying two or three areas for improvement (you should get these from your teacher's feedback). However, you may also be aware of these areas yourself once you have given your talk.

Top Tip

Do not just read your notes aloud – you are not being tested on your ability to read. A major aim is to talk in the most fluent and confident manner that you can.

Quick Test

1. Why would you use body language?
2. Why is it important to listen?
3. Why is it important to plan your talk?
4. Towards the end of your talk, what might you do to involve your audience?

Answers 1. It helps people to understand you and makes your speech more interesting. **2.** Conversations need listeners too; by listening, you can make better points. **3.** It helps to give a more coherent structure and improve the detail. **4.** Ask questions or show them props.

Test your progress

Use the questions to test your progress.
Check your answers at the back of the book on page 95.

1. What are the two modes of talk that are assessed?

   ....

2. How is listening assessed?

   ....

3. State three potential purposes for a solo talk?

   ....

4. Briefly explain what is meant by 'body language'.

   ....

5. What is 'register' in speech?

   ....

6. Explain what is meant by 'irony'.

   ....

7. Why is it important to listen?

   ....

8. What kinds of assignments are suitable for discussing, arguing and persuading?

   ....

9. Why is it important that you do not write out long passages for your talk?

   ....

10. What is meant by 'structure' in a talk?

    ....

11. Why is it important to self-assess after your talk?

    ....

12. A good talk is almost always:
    a) about an interesting subject
    b) well-structured and prepared
    c) funny
    d) informative.

13. Brainstorming is:
    a) a good method of structuring your talk
    b) a good way of planning your talk
    c) a good way of discussing a topic
    d) a good way of producing ideas for your talk.

14. A good way to give a fluent talk is:

    a) to write it out completely and learn it off by heart

    b) to make sure it has a beginning, middle and end

    c) to write key phrases on pieces of cards as prompts

    d) to choose a subject you know really well.

15. Which of the following is the most important factor when delivering a successful talk?

    a) Matching the subject of your talk with your audience.

    b) Providing opportunities for audience interaction.

    c) Standing up straight.

    d) Appearing relaxed and confident.

Well … the … the island in 'Lord of the Flies' is a sort of laboratory that William Golding has set up. It's like he said, 'What would happen if a group of boys was … were stranded on a desert island. He couldn't find out by putting a group of real boys on a real island so he wrote the novel as a … thought experiment. He decided on that … and he let things take their course as any scientist would. Once the boys were up and running – or not as the case may be – he introduced new elements to the basic formula to see what would happen.

So … the biggest challenge he gave the kids was the beast. It's interesting, innit, that the beast appeared in the boys' heads before it was given form by the dead parachutist. What I'm saying is that the beast is really the boys' fear an all … all the things that go wrong on the island are 'cause of fear.

This … is bad news for the rest of us. Golding reckons that fcar is what makes any group of people hostile and aggressive. Just as the boys on the island can't get on because of fear … peoples in the world can't get on because of fear. It's no coincidence, is it, that the boys are stranded on the island because the adults are having a nuclear war. Er … that's it.

Question 16.

Here is a transcript of part of a talk given by a student. Read it carefully and then make five suggestions that would improve the speech.

How did you do?

    1–5   correct ……………… start again

    6–10 correct ……………… getting there

    11–16 correct ……………… excellent

Exam technique

The importance of the exam

Although two-thirds of you final grade is already decided, and hopefully you will have worked hard on your folio and talk assessments, the examination is still very important. This is especially true because of the way that **your folio grade and your exam grade are combined**. In effect, the two are 'rounded-up' when they don't average out to a full number. For example, a Grade 3 in your Reading folio and a Grade 2 in your Reading exam would combine to give you an overall Grade 2 for Reading. The same rule applies to the Writing exam.

It is possible, therefore, to **significantly boost your coursework grades by good examination performance**.

Managing your time

- The secret of success is to **do a little and often every day**. Assign yourself set times to do your revision. Why not stick to the times you would have used to attend your English lessons in school?
- Get together with a friend – you will help to motivate each other.
- Improve your proof-reading skills by marking the work of friends.
- Managing your time is crucial in exams. Allow yourself **five to ten minutes to check your work through for errors** of sense, spelling and punctuation. Ask yourself, 'What errors do I usually make?'

Top Tip

Use your time effectively.

Close reading exams

- Do not panic! Channel all your nervous energy and adrenaline into your exam.
- Do not be late. Each paper lasts for 50 minutes so if you are even five minutes late you will have lost 10 per cent of your time.
- Read through Close Reading passages twice: firstly to get the gist of the meaning and then for deeper understanding. Carefully read the passages and note the development of arguments and ideas as well as how they are expressed by underlining words, using a highlighter, or by making short, phrase-like notes.
- Use the paragraph references given to save wasting time.
- Do not give up! The questions do not get harder as you work through them, so even if you have found one section difficult, you may find the next page less so.

Top Tip

Read page 79 for more pointers about Close Reading.

Read carefully

Everyone tends to rush the Close Reading paper. At 50 minutes it is a tight exam, but you have enough time to tackle the task thoroughly. The key to success is not getting the questions answered – it's getting them correct! And this will not happen unless the passage has been understood. This will require **careful reading of the passage**. Pay particular attention to the topic sentences as these will form the backbone of the text.

Remember to scan through the questions between your first and second reading of the passage, as they will indicate the key areas of the passage.

Warning!

You will come across questions that offer either zero marks or two marks: 0 2. It is vital that you do enough to earn both marks in your answer as there is no half-way house. Many candidates get half the answer correct for this type of question but end up with no mark as the marker can only award zero or full marks. You will need to make two points in your answer or to make a point and then explain it more fully.

Quick Test

Here is an example from a recent General Paper:

'On the twenty-fourth of June, in the year 1914, a young man went into a house, and never came out again. His name was William Walter Gordon Maitland, aged twenty-two, of 14, Elliesland Street, Milhall, in the county of Lanarkshire and one summer afternoon he vanished from the face of the earth. It was as simple, and as complicated as that.'

1. What happened to William Maitland on 24 June, 1914? (0 2)

2. The writer describes the event as being 'as simple, and as complicated as that'.
   a) Why do you think the writer calls it 'simple'? (0 2)
   b) Why do you think the writer calls it 'complicated'? (0 2)

These questions are all 'two marks or zero' type questions. It is important not to simply write down the most obvious part of the answer and then leave it at that, as this would result in zero marks.

For example, if your answer to Question 1 was 'He disappeared', you would score no marks. Similarly, if you said, 'He went into a house', you would score zero marks. If you realised that to gain two marks you need to make two points and you wrote, 'He went into a house and disappeared', you would gain the full two marks.

Now try Question 2 for yourself.

Answers 2. a) It was simple because the facts are straightforward and going into a house is an ordinary thing to do.
b) It was complicated because there is no obvious explanation for what had happened and the whole incident is very mysterious.

Close reading

What you have to do

All candidates will sit two close reading papers. Everyone sits the General Paper, and will then sit either the Credit Paper or the Foundation Paper. Each exam is 50 minutes long and there will be approximately the same number of questions at each level.

The reading passages are designed to test your **close reading skills**; that is, **your ability to understand the writer's meaning and purpose and the way that he or she uses language**. They may be any type of writing (newspaper article, prose extract, advertising, etc.).

Foundation

The Foundation Paper covers Grades 5 and 6. At this level you can expect to read texts that are relatively **straightforward** in content and which relate to personal interests and experience. The presentation of ideas will be clear and the language uncomplicated. Many of the questions will focus on basic understanding and the retrieval of information.

General

The General Paper will contain a **greater degree of difficulty** than the Foundation Paper, but will still be accessible, on the whole, to a competent reader. Some questions on how the writer has used language are likely to feature at this level.

Credit

The Credit Paper contains **content that is challenging** and which goes beyond what would be regarded as immediately accessible. This means that you will have to work to understand the full meaning of the passage. The language is liable to be **complex** and ideas may be **more abstract** than in the other levels. Accordingly, the questions themselves will be of a **more sophisticated** nature.

What the questions are testing

It will help if you understand what the questions are designed to do. Questions are constructed to test your abilities in the following areas:

- **Reading to gain an overall impression or gist of a text** – questions here will test your general understanding of a passage.

- **Reading to obtain particular information from a text** – here you will be looking for specific bits of information such as facts.

- **Reading to grasp ideas and feelings** – this area is more difficult because it is more abstract; however, it is essentially testing your understanding of how language is used.

- **Reading to evaluate the writer's attitudes, assumptions and arguments** – perhaps the most difficult area; clearly you have to understand the passage thoroughly in order to make judgement on its effectiveness and arguments.

- **Reading to appreciate the writer's craft** – this area deals with how the writer has used language, e.g. structure, vocabulary, figurative language, punctuation (all the techniques we suggested you should use in your own writing!).

Some suggestions for tackling close reading

- At a minimum, **read the passage carefully** and then **scan through the questions**. Re-read the passage before tackling any answers.

- **Pay attention to the marks on offer** as this will indicate the number of points required in your answer. Generally speaking, one mark will require one point to be made so if there is a 2-mark answer, make sure that you are either making two points or making one point and then explaining it.

- As with the marks, **the space provided in the answer booklet is a guide as to the length** of answer required. If there is a single line and you find yourself writing a paragraph, you are probably saying too much. However, if there are three lines provided and your answer only fills half of one line, you are not answering fully enough.

- The words '**write down**' or '**quote**' in the question mean that you can lift your answer straight from the passage.

- **Answer clearly and concisely**. You are not required to write in sentences unless you have been asked to 'explain' or 'describe' something.

- '**Explain fully**' indicates that you should be using your own words.

- **Consider the context** of any words or phrases where you are unsure of the meaning. Context simply means the sentences around a particular word and it will often help you to work out the meaning.

- If searching a particular paragraph for a word or phrase, **eliminate the obvious** and then **consider the remainder** – it may be the answer!

- **Do not leave blank spaces**. Wrong answers do not lose marks.

Hunter of Dryburn

Brian McCabe

Close reading test paper

The following passage is an extract from Sean Coughlan's article, **The Inside Story, Climate Change – Global Warming** (The Times, 13th February).

A passage of this complexity would appear in a Credit level exam.

Read through the whole passage first, to get the gist of its main ideas. Then go back and try the questions on each section.

An explanation of the answers follows each mini-section.

Top Tip

Remember that in the exam, all the questions will follow the passage, although they will be organised to focus on sections at a time.

Global warning

Why are governments so paralysed in the face of catastrophic climate change? Sean Coughlan examines the facts and the arguments.

1. When an international team of researchers announced that climate change could kill a quarter of the species of plants and creatures currently sharing the planet with us, it was a figure so stark that the issue of global warming made headlines around the world.

2. Scientists had studied six different regions and had constructed computer models to investigate how more than 1,100 different species would survive the temperature changes that will accompany global warming. 'If the projections can be extrapolated globally, and to other groups of land animals and plants, our analyses suggest that well over a million species could be threatened with extinction as a result of climate change,' said the lead author of the research, Chris Thomas.

3. Variety of flowers in Africa, lizards in Australia and birds in Scotland could be swept away by a climate change triggered by the emission of 'greenhouse gases' into the atmosphere. And the timescale is not a distant point on the horizon; we could have extinguished many types of life on Earth by 2050.

Climate change is triggered by the emission of 'greenhouse gases' into the environment.

4. As a mid-range forecast, researchers found that the effect of climate changes would spell the end for 25 per cent of species – rising to 37 per cent on a more pessimistic projection – and the damage already in progress would lead to the extinction of 18 per cent of species.

5. Is this apocalyptic vision really going to happen? Is there a scientific consensus? And even if we wanted to limit global warming, is there any realistic chance of international cooperation?

Questions

Look at paragraphs 1–5.

1. Why did the issue of global warming make headlines around the world? *(2 marks)*

    ....

    ....

    ....

    ....

2. Explain how the writer conveys the global nature and scale of the danger posed. *(2 marks)*

    ....

    ....

    ....

    ....

3. How does the use of statistics in paragraph 4 help you to understand the meaning of 'pessimistic'? *(2 marks)*

    ....

    ....

    ....

    ....

4. What does the phrase 'apocalyptic vision' suggest? *(2 marks)*

    ....

    ....

    ....

    ....

Answers

1. i) One mark for explaining that the research suggested a major problem – statistic 'a quarter of the species'.
    ii) One mark for gloss on 'stark' suggesting that the danger was a very real threat.
2. i) 'over a million species' – candidate should really suggest the vast scale suggested by this figure.
    ii) Reference in paragraph 3 to different countries to suggest global nature of the problem.
3. i) One mark for explaining that 'pessimistic' means to take a negative view of things.
    ii) The statistics suggest the worst case scenario, 'rising to 37 per cent', indicating an even worse position than might be the the case. This suggests the meaning of taking a negative view.
4. A view of the future that suggests destruction and death.

Close reading passage continued ...

6. Environmental campaigners in Greenpeace are in no doubt about the extent of the danger, identifying climate change as the biggest single environmental threat to the planet. But spokesperson Ben Stewart says that the scale of the problem is such that people can feel overwhelmed – frozen in the headlights as we watch the juggernaut hurtling nearer. 'It seems as though, even when people accept that there is a huge problem, we don't feel we have the ability to do anything.'

7. But Ben Stewart believes that the message is getting through – and that the international decision taken at the Kyoto conference in 1992 to cut emissions was a cause for optimism, even though the US Government has not ratified the deal. If action is taken to ratify greenhouse emissions, he says, it won't be a moment too soon. He quotes research from the World Health Organisation which claimed that global warming was already causing the deaths of tens of thousands of people, through destruction of agriculture and the spread of diseases. He also raised the spectre of 'climate refugees', where large numbers of people will be pushed out of their own land because of global warming and will have to look for asylum elsewhere.

8. But if we are looking for a reason why there has not been urgent and immediate action to stop such a nightmare vision of the future, then we have to take a step back and see that the arguments on global warming are not cast in black and white. Scientists are far from unanimous about the cause or ultimate effect of global warming. There are also more immediate economic arguments over cutting emissions that are being held in the balance against scientific forecasts. And if it's a question of losing jobs tomorrow, or worrying about something that might happen in fifty years, then politicians are under pressure to act in the short-term.

Questions continued ...

Look at paragraphs 6–8.

5. 'frozen in the headlights as we watch the juggernaut hurtling nearer'.

   a) Explain fully the image being used here. *(2 marks)*

   ....

   ....

   ....

   ....

   b) How does it relate to the rest of the paragraph? *(2 marks)*

   ....

   ....

   ....

   ....

6. What reservation is expressed about the decision taken at the Kyoto conference to cut emissions? *(1 mark)*

   ....

   ....

7. **a)** Using your own words, explain how global warming is causing death. *(2 marks)*

   ....

   ....

   ....

   ....

   b) What other 'problem' is likely to be caused by global warming? *(2 marks)*

   ....

   ....

   ....

   ....

8. Explain clearly the situation that politicians find themselves in. *(2 marks)*

   ....

   ....

   ....

   ....

Answers

5. **a)** The image is that of an animal mesmerised by the headlamps of an approaching lorry and unable to escape as a result.
   b) It links with the final sentence which indicates that even though we know that there is a big issue about global warming to be tackled, we don't feel able to actually do anything about it.

6. The reservation is that the US has not signed up to the agreement – 'even though the US Government has not ratified the deal'.

7. **a)** The answer lies in the phrase 'through the destruction of agriculture and the spread of diseases', but this has to be put into the candidate's own words, i.e. through plants and crops being ruined, causing hunger, and through illnesses being passed on.
   b) Global warming is likely to force people to abandon their homes because of the changed climate, and they will then have to find somewhere else to live – 'climate refugees'.

8. Politicians are forced to act on problems now rather than ones that will only have an impact in the future.

Inverted commas – speech

Inverted commas are used to **mark off direct speech**, where they are placed around the actual words spoken: for example in paragraph 6 'It seems as though, even when people accept that there is a huge problem, we don't feel we have the ability to do anything.'

Close reading passage continued ...

9. In Britain, Joe Buchdahl, coordinator of the Atmosphere, Climate and Environment Information Programme, puts forward the mainstream 'official' view. The project is supported by the Department for Environment, Food and Rural Affairs (DEFRA) to present unbiased and balanced information about global warming.

10. Buchdahl says that there is now a 'balance of evidence' which confirms the climate is changing – and that, increasingly, it is believed that there is a 'human fingerprint' on these changes.

11. The British Government reported its belief that global temperature rises 'cannot be explained by natural factors' and the evidence suggests that 'increasing greenhouse gas levels due to human activities are largely responsible'. As a result, it concluded that Britain in the short term is likely to face hotter, drier summers and warmer wetter winters. In the long term (perhaps within 200 years) it is predicted the effect will be quite the opposite – global warming may prematurely usher in a new ice age for the UK.

12. The British Isles draws its geographically misplaced warmth from the Gulf Stream, a 'conveyor belt' for warm water and consequently humid air, which originates in the Gulf of Mexico and passes through the North Atlantic. The Gulf Stream relies on a strong undercurrent of cold water, cooled by the polar ice cap.

13. Global warming is causing this 'continent-size' body of ice to melt, pouring massive amounts of fresh water into the North Atlantic. This weakens the Gulf Stream and, some scientists predict, will push it south and out of Britain's waters. No warm water would mean, while the rest of the world bakes, the region around the British Isles will literally freeze.

Inverted commas – quotations

Inverted commas are used to indicate when a **quotation** is being used: in paragraph 11, for example, it talks about the British Government reporting its belief that global temperature rises 'cannot be explained by natural factors'. As the British Government cannot actually speak, as such, this is a quotation either from a written report or from a speech by a spokesperson.

Questions continued ...

Look at paragraphs 9–13.

9. Using your own words, explain the key function of the Atmosphere, Climate, and Environment Information Group. *(2 marks)*

....

....

....

....

10. What does the phrase 'balance of evidence' mean? *(2 marks)*

....

....

....

....

11. What impact does the 'Gulf Stream' have on Britain's climate? *(1 mark)*

....

....

12. What long term consequence does Britain face as a result of global warming? *(1 mark)*

....

....

Answers

9. The answer lies in the phrase 'to present unbiased and balanced information', but this must be put into the candidate's own words; i.e. to provide opinion-free information from both sides of the argument.

10. It means an overall judgement based on considering the evidence from both sides of the debate.

11. It heats it up.

12. We might return to the ice age.

Close reading passage continued ...

14. But all of this doesn't necessarily mean that global warming will have the cataclysmic consequences that some scientists have suggested, says Joe Buchdahl. And he says that best-guesses should not be confused with something that will definitely happen. 'We don't know how well or badly humans and other species would adapt to changed climates and there are too many unpredictable factors to be certain about where global warming might lead.'

15. This is an international argument – and he says that we have to take seriously how the debate is perceived from other countries. If global emissions are to be cut, then the role of the US as the world's biggest economy will be vital. And in the US there are powerful lobbyists such as within the oil industry, who suggest that threats of global warning are overstated and that any hurried action could damage the economy without delivering any proven benefit.

16. There are also lobbyists in the US who argue that, rather than cutting emission, the answer lies in developing cleaner technology.

Questions continued ...

Look at paragraphs 14–16.

13. Which phrase in paragraph 8 suggests a similar meaning to cataclysmic?   *(2 marks)*

....

....

....

....

14. Using your own words, explain why we cannot be certain as to what will happen in the future.   *(2 marks)*

....

....

....

....

15. a) Why is the position of the US so vital to the international debate about what should happen?   *(1 marks)*

....

....

b) What reservations do some US commentators have? *(2 marks)*

....

....

....

....

c) What alternative strategy to cutting emissions is suggested? *(1 marks)*

....

....

d) What might you infer about the role of 'lobbyists' from the oil industry? *(2 marks)*

....

....

....

....

Inverted commas – titles

Inverted commas can be used to **indicate the title** of something, such as a book: 'Stone Cold'. Increasingly, however, titles are being indicated by the use of italics: *Stone Cold*.

Answers

13. A nightmare vision of the future.

14. We don't know how animals and humans might change owing to climate changes. There are too many uncertainties involved to be certain what might happen.

15. a) It is the world's biggest economy.

b) That the threat has been exaggerated and that quick solutions might do more damage without actually working.

c) Cleaner technology

d) That they have a powerful voice and may have a vested interest because oil is one of the main sources of gas emissions.

Close reading passage continued ...

17. But if there is growing agreement that the climate is changing, the next big question is how we should respond. What action should we take to either delay or offset the effects? This is the challenge being taken up by a network of 200 scientists who are working on scientific responses to global warming.

18. Asher Minns, speaking on behalf of the group, says that as well as trying to cut emissions, we should be looking at how we are going to adapt to a different type of climate. For instance, if the sea level is going to rise, which parts of the coastline do we want to protect, and which will we abandon? In a relatively affluent country such as Britain, such adaptations can be made and cities beside the sea protected. But he says there needs to be advanced planning for countries such as Bangladesh, where vast numbers of people will be susceptible to sea-level changes.

19. If there are going to be more violent storms, what will it mean for developed and non-developed countries? Who will pick up the bill for the damage? Who will look after the homeless? What will happen to people living on low-lying islands which become uninhabitable?

20. There will also be adaptations to be made by agriculture, he says. A warmer climate in Britain could mean a longer growing season and for some produce, the prospect of two crops a year instead of one. But on the downside, milder weather will mean that pests and diseases are not killed off by the frost in winter.

Melting of the polar ice-caps and resulting rise in sea level will threaten many coastal cities.

Varying sentence structure

Sentences normally **begin with a subject** (the person or thing doing whatever action is being described) **followed by a verb, predicate** (the action being done). When this order is changed the writer is usually trying to create a particular effect.

Look back to the last sentence in paragraph 11, for example. This would normally be written 'It is predicted the effect will be quite the opposite in the long term (perhaps within 200 years)...

By placing the phrase 'In the long term' at the beginning of the sentence the writer is drawing attention to the timescale we are dealing with, emphasising the potentially serious consequences. (In this case it also links effectively with the previous sentence, which dealt with the 'short term' issues.)

Recognising when a sentence is structured differently from the normal pattern can assist with understanding the writer's craft and purpose.

Questions continued ...

Look at paragraphs 17–20.

16. Using your own words, explain fully the three examples used to illustrate the need to adapt to climate change.

a) ....

....

....

.... *(2 marks)*

b) ....

....

....

.... *(2 marks)*

c) ....

....

....

.... *(2 marks)*

Repetition

Repetition is a technique used by writers often to create a sense of **emphasis**. In paragraph 19 we see a series of questions being posed to create a dramatic impact and to suggest the large number of issues that require to be addressed.

Answers

16. a) From paragraph 18: The sea is getting higher because of global warming and this will mean that some seaside areas, including towns, will be under threat. In rich countries it might be possible to protect some areas but poorer countries will be badly affected without some help.

b) From paragraph 19: Changes to the weather will mean more damage being done and this will create problems such as people losing their homes.

c) Farming will change with some good effects, such as more harvests, but the lack of a cold winter will mean that insects will survive and possibly cause problems.

Close reading passage continued ...

21. But Asher Minns is in no doubt that such climate change is taking place – and that we need to face up to making a decision about making a response.

22. So where has the argument over global warming reached? In a relatively short space of time, it has become an internationally recognised issue.

23. But a consensus on the extent of the likely impact or causes of global warming remains elusive. The US, the biggest producer of greenhouse gases, remains the strongest sceptic when it comes to adopting an internationally-enforced process for reducing emissions. What is certain is that, whatever happens, the heat won't be going out of this argument for many years to come.

Inverted commas – non-literal meanings

Often when a word is used in a **non-literal** fashion, it is marked off by inverted commas. This is to indicate to the reader that the writer is aware of **the non-conventional use of the word** and wants you to understand its purpose.

Look back to paragraph 12, for example. Here, 'conveyor-belt' is in inverted commas because we are not meant to think that there is an actual conveyor belt operating. They are used to indicate that the Gulf Stream acts like a conveyor belt, carrying the warm water along its predetermined course like a conveyor belt in a factory carrying goods or parts.

Parenthesis

Parenthesis is where **additional information** is provided in a sentence which tells us more but which is **not essential** to the main point of the sentence. It can be indicated by **brackets, dashes**, or by **a pair of commas**.

In paragraph 23, for example, parenthesis is used to indicate that the US is 'the biggest producer of greenhouse gases'. This is an important fact, but if we took it out of the sentence we would still be left with the main point – that 'the US remains the strongest sceptic when it come to adopting an internationally enforced process for reducing emissions.'

Parenthesis is often used to **allow the writer to add a personal comment** while still presenting the facts.

Questions continued ...

Look at paragraphs 21–23.

17. 'But a consensus ...' Why has the writer chosen to begin a new paragraph with the above phrase, rather than using 'but' to join the new sentence to the preceding one?

....

....

....

.... *(2 marks)*

18. How effective do you consider the final paragraph to be in summing up the article?

....

....

....

.... *(2 marks)*

Statistics

It is important to remember that statistics are primarily numbers. The **context** in which they are used **is crucial** as to how we should interpret them.

For example if we said that 'one hundred people turned up at the meeting' – we have a bald statistic. Is that a high number or a low one? If, however, we said. 'As many as one hundred people attended the meeting', we are indicating that this is a significant figure by our use of the phrase 'as many as'. On the other hand, 'Only one hundred people turned up at the meeting', would downplay the level of the problem.

Context is key to understanding statistics.

Literal and non-literal meanings

Words have literal and non-literal meanings and it is important to recognise the difference.

When a word is used **literally** it **means exactly what it says**: 'The knife was very sharp' – 'sharp' means, here, that it has an edge to it that might cut you.

If we said, 'The teacher has a very sharp brain', we are not suggesting that the physical brain is honed to an edge but simply that the teacher is clever and quick witted. 'Sharp' is being used in a non-literal sense here to make an association that we can understand.

Answers

17. If he hadn't used 'but' it would have made sense, but by separating it off and making it the start of a new paragraph, he has emphasised the difficulty of getting agreement.

18. It is effective because it highlights the main difficulty outlined in the passage and it also has a play-on-words – 'the heat won't be going out of this argument' – which links with the passage's topic of global warming.

Writing

Choosing a task

Top Tip
Most of the assignments have a **visual stimulus** and a **general guide** – make use of these to help you tune in to the task.

In the exam you will have a wide choice of topics to choose from. It is important that you **make your choice quickly and appropriately**.

Try to have a **clear idea of the type of task that you are looking for**. If you are good at personal experience essays and not so good at short stories, for example, this should guide your choice of question.

Ask yourself the following questions as you consider the options:

1: Am I interested in this subject?

You will produce better work if you are writing about something in which you have a real interest as the **genuine** nature of your response will shine through.

2: Do I know enough about it?

Remember that being interested in something is not the same as knowing about it. You will find it difficult to write enough to justify a good grade if your **basic knowledge** is inadequate.

3: Can I write in the style required?

Be clear about the style of essay being asked for: **personal experience**, **argumentative**, **descriptive** or **short story**. Be especially careful about special registers such as a speech or radio script – if you are not experienced in the style being asked for it would be better to make another choice. **Writing in the wrong genre may be heavily punished**.

If the answer is 'Yes' to all three of the above questions, you can tackle the task with confidence.

Attaining a high grade

You will need to do the following to produce a good answer.

Plan your writing – at a minimum use a mind-map to generate some ideas.

Show **accuracy** in your spelling and punctuation.

Have a sound structure to your work, using **well-constructed paragraphs** with topic sentences.

Use **varied sentence structure** and **punctuation**, as well as showing **clarity** of thought.

Focus on your purpose.

Proof-read your work and **correct it where necessary**. Teachers and examiners love to see evidence of proof-reading because it shows that pupils have attained a level of maturity as independent learners.

Relevance

A **common mistake** made in the exam is for the candidate to **write the wrong type of essay**. This will almost always lead to a poorer grade and in some instances could result in a Grade 7 being awarded.

Consider the following example:

> Young people like to assert their independence from parents through their sense of fashion, their taste in music, their choice of friends. Discuss the relevance of this statement to today's youth.

The word '**discuss**' tells you that this is a **discursive essay**. However, the temptation might be to treat it as a personal experience type essay and this would lead to a poorer grade.

You must read the task carefully.

If you are invited to write in any way you choose about a topic – make sure that you <u>do</u> choose and that you have a particular style of essay in mind. The marker should be able to see clearly, for example, where an essay is about a personal experience as opposed to being a creative short story.

Where you are given a title to use, make sure that **the idea suggested by the title is central to your essay** and not simply an awkward twist at the end, as this would not justify its relevance.

Caution!

One major difference between the folio and the exam is that **in the exam you do not have the opportunity to re-draft your work**.

However, **the same standard of marking applies with regard to punctuation, paragraphing and spelling**. Take extra care, therefore, to punctuate and paragraph accurately. A significant number of missing full stops, for example, will pull an otherwise good essay down to a Grade 4 or less. And if you fail to structure your essay effectively with good paragraphing, you will again be looking at Grade 4 as your maximum.

Check over your work carefully. If you realise that you should have started a new paragraph use the symbols NP in the margin to indicate this to the marker.

Top Tip

Use Past Papers for exam practice to get a feel for how they are laid out and for the type of questions you may be asked.

> This book will have helped you maximise your folio and talk grades and prepared you well for the examination. Now go to the Leckie and Leckie Past Papers for more exam practice. **Good luck!**

Answers

Writing skills (pages 24–25)

Punctuation and sentences

1. You need to punctuate your work so that your readers will fully understand your meaning.
2. Check your answer against page 7. (Award yourself a mark if you got all five.)
3. Jemma, *Great Expectations*, English, the first She, Charles Dickens and Easter.
4. Full stop, semi-colon, colon, exclamation mark and question mark.
5. They join closely-related sentences; they separate sets of items in lists when there are commas within the sets or lists.
6. A question to which you do not expect a direct answer; you expect instead that your listener will agree with you.
7. Colons can introduce a list; they can introduce a sentence which expands upon the meaning of the first sentence; they can also introduce long quotations that are separated from the writer's prose.
8. Inverted commas are needed for words spoken; the speech needs to be separated from the rest of the writing by a punctuation mark; it is introduced with a capital letter; you need a new line for each speaker; and each new line should be indented three spaces from the margin.
9. Apostrophes can indicate possession or an abbreviated word or phrase.
10. Before the 's' as with the firemen's equipment.
11. Statements, exclamations, instructions or commands and questions.
12. The main clause is 'I will go to the cinema'. The dependent clause is 'as soon as I have done the washing up'.

Spelling and expression

13. Spelling phonetically sounding out each syllable:
   - Look–Say–Cover–Write–Check
   - Use a dictionary; produce a mnemonic.
14. It is 'i' before 'e' except after 'c'.
15. There is a consonant before the 'y' as with 'city'; so it is 'cities'.
16. There is a vowel before the 'y' as with 'monkey'; so it is 'monkeys'.
17. They are all to do with place.
18. Beginning, appearance, interested, grammar, tongue, definitely, necessity, rhythm, sentence.
19. Synonyms are words that mean the same.
20. Homophones are words that are different yet sound the same. For instance, 'whether' and 'weather'.
21. Connective words link phrases, sentences and paragraphs together.
22. To help signpost ideas and arguments so that readers can follow what you mean.
23. Paragraphs break up forbidding chunks of text and make meaning clear. Writers need them to organise their main points and ideas.
24. The topic sentence is the main sentence in a paragraph. The remaining sentences expand on its meaning.
25. 'Control' is the ability to write sentences and paragraphs of appropriate length with control over expression. Word choices and punctuation will also be appropriate and accurate.
26. Because.
27. The opening line of Tennyson's poem 'The Eagle' is very striking.
   'He clasps the crag with crooked hands.'
   The most noticeable thing about it is the use of the word 'hands' where the reader might have expected something like 'talons' or 'claws'. The second thing that makes the line striking is the alliteration on the letter 'c'. The repeated 'c's give the line a harsh sound which is in keeping with the eagle's harsh environment.

Writing (pages 34–35)

1. Two
2. As appropriate to task but usually between 600–800 words.
3. Functional style writing.
4. Personal writing.
5. Creative writing, e.g. short story, poetry, drama.
6. Informative piece; biography; opinion type essay; discursive.
7. A personal experience; a short story; a poem.
8. To allow your personality to shine through.
9. Revealing what you have learned or gained from a situation.
10. Your writing may become clichéd.
11. Your writing will be more genuine and therefore more effective.
12. Use statistics; compare and contrast; use an anecdote; give an example.
13. The use of 'as' or 'like' in the comparison.
14. To make your writing more descriptive and interesting.
15. An interesting beginning which draws the reader in.
16. The setting is where the story is supposed to be in time and place.
17. First and third person.
18. Third person.
19. The plan or outline of the story.
20. Notes, brainstorm or spidergram.
21. Fluency of expression and punctuation
22. Linear is a 'straight line'. There is no going backwards or forwards as the story unfolds. For example, *Romeo and Juliet* is a linear play because the action takes place over four days.
23. So that you are looking from at least two sides of a topic.
24. You can get information from knowledgeable people, libraries, the Internet, encyclopedias, companies, embassies, etc.
25. No.
26. Poetry, dramascript.
27. Yes.
28. To read over your work, checking for and correcting mistakes.
29. In the writing exam.

Reading: Responding to Literature (pages 40–41)

Question A

1. c
2. b
3. c
4. a

Question B

Sailor speech shows that they can't directly change fate

Temptation – Use the truth against him, Thane of Cawdor greeting is true when they utter it

Witches diagram

Conclusion

Temptation 2 – All three warnings are true. Just not what Macbeth expected

Effect on Lady Macbeth – Letter describes meeting – she persuades Macbeth

Effect on Macbeth – Witches not present at murder – his decision

Question C

Give yourself marks out of 10 – one mark for each point you have made. Have someone check your work.

Answers

Reading: Prose (pages 48–49)

1. The outline or structure of a piece of writing.
2. To explain what is different.
3. This refers to the kind or type of writing; for example: romance, adventure, detective, horror, etc.
4. How the writer creates effects through emotive or figurative writing.
5. Saying one thing while meaning another, or speaking the truth without knowing it.
6. Connectives which allow you to move from one argument or point to another in a fluent manner. They are often key words or phrases that are needed at the beginning of paragraphs, such as 'similarly' or 'on the other hand'.
7. First and third person.
8. He or she uses 'I' because they are in the story.
9. Not necessarily – do not confuse author with narrator.
10. Usually the third person. You can have a third-person omniscient all-seeing narrator.
11. Any of the ways set out on 'What to look for in characters' on page 43 will do for this answer.
12. An all-knowing author, usually in third-person stories.
13. Round characters develop because they change in the course of the novel. Flat characters do not change, thus they do not develop.
14. 'Conversation' – two people speaking.
15. Dialogue makes characters vivid and lifelike. What characters say reveals their motives and personality traits; readers can learn about characters from what other characters say about them.
16. New speaker, new line and indent; begin with a capital letter; introduce with a punctuation mark and use inverted commas.
17. A character speaking alone.
18. The answer is similar to that for question 15.
19. Both have: plots, stories, dialogue, characters, themes and ideas.
20. Short stories tend to concentrate on one incident, with one plot and fewer themes and a shorter time-span for the action; there are also fewer characters with less detail; the dialogue is more fragmented; description in short stories is more economical.
21. There is not enough space to do otherwise.
22. Through description; the use of imagery; variety in language and sentences; the tone of the narrator and his or her closeness to the action.
23. The choice of words chosen by the author.
24. True.
25. True.
26. False.
27. Alliteration is the repetition of initial consonants in words for an effect; assonance is the repetition of similar vowel sounds in words for an effect.
28. The main idea or message of a story.

Reading: drama (pages 58–59)

Structure and theme

1. Check your answers against page 52.
2. Comment on them.
3. History, Tragedy and Comedy. There is a sub-genre: Tragicomedy.
4. Poetic verse, blank verse and prose.
5. For the end of scenes and scenes of dramatic intensity.
6. To show dignified speech; speech that helps convey feeling and mood.
7. A sense of normality and order. 'All is well with the world'.
8. Problems are introduced and order begins to break down.
9. The point of highest dramatic intensity before the protagonist's fall.
10. Battles, unmasking, deaths, marriages, etc.
11. Order is restored and the right people are back in control.12.A central idea or ideas.
13. Check your answers with those in 'Themes' on page 53. There are also other themes.
14. Love, appearance and reality, good and evil, identity and disguise, etc.
15. A comic scene is followed by a serious scene.
16. This makes a scene appear even more intense or light-hearted because of the contrasting emotions of the previous scene.
17. Self-knowledge is the ability to learn from your faults when others point them out to you. Characters who do so 'develop'.
18. Order – problems – chaos – climax – resolution with new order.

Imagery

19. Any kind of imagery or decorative language with alliteration, etc.
20. A comparison using 'as' or 'like'; for example, 'Clare is like a flower'.
21. It is a comparison which implies or states that something is something else: 'Clare is a flower'.
22. A metaphor that runs or is 'extended' over several lines or a scene.
23. It means 'person-making'. It is powerful metaphor in which things or ideas are given human traits for an enhanced literary effect.
24. Two opposite terms yoked together for effect; for example, 'A Hard Day's Night'.
25. A character, theme or image that recurs.
26. Imagery helps to say more about points made in dialogue and action. It reinforces and enhances the audience's ideas of the characters. It can magnify or draw attention to themes or issues in the text.
27. Characters speak with irony when they say something that is truer than they realise.
28. It is dramatically ironic when the audience knows something important that characters do not. Sometimes this is complicated by one character knowing what another does with the audience sharing their knowledge.
29. Passages and scenes of dramatic intensity. An example is where Romeo first speaks with Juliet.
30. It includes figurative language, including word-pictures like similes and metaphors.

Reading: poetry (pages 68–69)

1. Maximum of two.
2. Reading.
3. Free-verse, quatrains, couplets, sonnets, etc.
4. The attitude of the narrator to his or her topic and to the reader.
5. First and third person.
6. True.
7. A key message or idea.
8. False – it is a stanza.
9. False – it is a simile.
10. A run-on line. Poets use them for effect.
11. To 'compare' is to note what is similar; to 'contrast' is to explain what is different.
12. A figure of speech and a paradox in which two contradictory terms are brought together for an effect: 'awfully nice' and 'alone together'.
13. Usually mixed feelings or a paradox.
14. True – they are composed of two couplets.
15. Stanzas of irregular length and number.
16. It is an ideal form for conversation and argument.
17. Repetition of vowel sounds for an effect.
18. At the end of your essay. Do give your views because examiners are interested in what you think.
19. Comment on it.
20. A picture created by the poet's use of language, which may suggest associations to the reader.

Talking (pages 74–75)

1. Individual and group.
2. Through your ability to respond to comments and questions from others.
3. Convey information; express ideas and opinions; relate a personal experience.
4. Non-verbal language such as eye contact, hand gestures, etc.
5. Register is the tone you adopt when addressing various audiences; for example, you should speak to a judge differently than you would speak to a friend.
6. We are being ironic if the tone of voice we use implies the opposite meaning of the words we use.
7. Good listeners have better, more complex conversations and good turn-taking skills.
8. Debates and topical issues in the news or an issue that came out of a class text.
9. You are assessed on your ability to talk, not to read. Long, written passages prevent fluency in speech because of the temptation to look at them for reassurance.
10. The 'structure' of your talk is the clarity and order of its presentation.
11. Self-assessment is crucial for setting new targets for improvement and achieving them.
12. b
13. d
14. c
15. a
16. Various answers: avoid hesitation suggested by the various ellipsis; don't use colloquialisms or slang, e.g. 'innit'; link points more effectively, e.g. 'So...'; avoid contractions, e.g. 'cause; conclude positively rather than trailing off, e.g. 'Er... that's it.'

Index

Text Credits

Leckie & Leckie is grateful to the copyright holders, as credited, for permission to use their material. Every effort has been made to trace the copyright holders and to obtain their permission for the use of copyright material. Leckie & Leckie will gladly receive information enabling them to rectify any error or omission in subsequent editions.

Page 45: 'Flight' from The Habit of Loving © 1957 Doris Lessing. Reprinted by kind permission of Jonathan Clowes Ltd., London, on behalf of Doris Lessing.

Page 45: extract from Superman and Paula Brown's New Snowsuit, Sylvia Plath © Faber and Faber.

Page 66: 'Six o'clock News' © Tom Leonard from Intimate Voices, Etruscan Books.

Page 66: by kind permission of John Agard c/o Caroline Sheldon Literary Agency 'Half Caste' from Get Back Pimple published by Puffin (1997).

Page 80: 'The Inside Story, Climate Change - Global Warning' from the Times Educational Supplement (Scotland), © Sean Coughlan.

Photo Credits

Page 80: 'Sugar beet refining factory' © Chris Knapton/Alamy

Page 84: 'Car exhaustion' © Bjorn Andren/Alamy

Page 88: 'Icebergs in an ice floe' © image100/Alamy

Pages 11, 13, 45, 50: images reproduced by kind permission of Topham Picture Point.